Informal
Assessments

BENCHMARK EDUCATION COMPANY

Informal Assessments for Grades K–6

Table of Contents

Assessment Introduction

In Benchmark Advance, daily teaching goes hand in hand with ongoing assessment and evaluation. The wide variety of informal literacy assessments provided in this resource enable teachers to:

- obtain multiple perspectives on the literacy growth occurring in their classrooms;
- monitor and reflect on their teaching and students' learning;
- make informed decisions about students' progress and needs;
- select appropriate materials and instructional techniques that match students' current level of development;
- document progress over time through a cumulative portfolio;
- report progress to students, parents, and administrators.

Meaningful, ongoing, and multifaceted observation is the heart of the evaluation process. Since observations must occur in authentic contexts, utilize your whole-class and small-group reading time to document students' efforts to: join collaborative conversations; ask and answer questions; react to prompts; contribute ideas for graphic organizers; process texts; problem-solve new words; apply targeted skills and strategies; act out and/or talk, draw, or write about books.

Use the information you gain to differentiate instruction by developmental reading behaviors and characteristics, metacognitive and comprehension strategy needs, instructional reading levels, fluency, and vocabulary understandings.

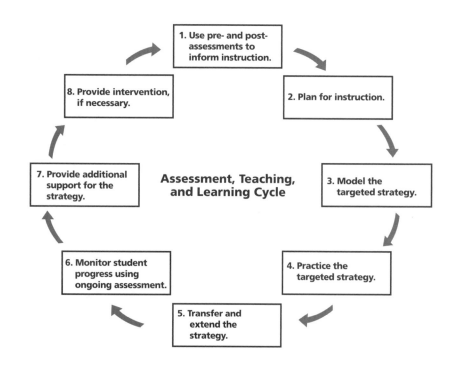

Assessment, Teaching, and Learning Cycle

1. Use pre- and post-assessments to inform instruction.
2. Plan for instruction.
3. Model the targeted strategy.
4. Practice the targeted strategy.
5. Transfer and extend the strategy.
6. Monitor student progress using ongoing assessment.
7. Provide additional support for the strategy.
8. Provide intervention, if necessary.

Rhodes and Shanklin (1993) outlined the eleven principles of literacy assessment. Each of these principles is supported in Benchmark Advance's informal assessments.

11 Principles of Literacy Assessment	How BEC Assessment Tools Support the Principles
1. Assess authentic reading and writing.	A variety of ongoing informal assessment tools are available for use before, during, and after literacy instruction.
2. Assess reading and writing in a variety of contexts.	Assessment tools can be administered one-on-one, in small groups, or with the whole class.
3. Assess the literacy environment, instruction, and students.	Assessment tools prompt teacher reflection and provide direction on linking assessment results to instruction.
4. Assess processes as well as products.	Rubrics and assessment tools are available for lesson analysis and noting observable developmental behaviors and characteristics.
5. Analyze error patterns in reading and writing.	Oral Reading Record Analysis forms and rubrics help identify error patterns, strengths, and needs.
6. Consider background knowledge in the assessment of reading and writing.	Student interest questionnaires and surveys gain insight into a student's literacy background and understanding.
7. Base assessment on normal developmental patterns and behavior in reading and writing.	A variety of reading behaviors and characteristics checklists are available to assist in noting developmental milestones and with reporting and planning during assessment meetings.
8. Clarify and use standards in the assessment of reading and writing.	Assessments are aligned with National Literacy Standards and state expectations for learning.
9. Use triangulation to corroborate data and make decisions.	Multiple assessments target different areas of literacy development and are designed to facilitate triangulation of data.
10. Involve students, parents, and other school personnel in the assessment process.	Sharing results from the Benchmark Education Assessments in data team meetings and parent conferences informs and involves others in the process of linking assessment and instruction.
11. Make assessment an ongoing part of everyday reading and writing opportunities and instruction.	Each assessment book provides guidance on how to schedule, manage, organize, and store assessments. Calendars and other planning tools are also provided.

Scheduling, Managing, Organizing, and Storing Assessments

Documenting progress through a cumulative portfolio is one of the greatest advantages of classroom-based assessment. Following are some tips to carry out this process in a teacher-friendly and student-friendly manner.

Scheduling Assessments

Use some assessments as pre- and post-evaluations of growth and development, completing them at the beginning and end of the school year. Conduct other assessments on a more frequent basis as needed. Assess informally during literacy activities every day. Schedule an individual literacy conference with each student every month, and use the information in instructional planning. Hold additional reading and writing conferences as needed to meet students' immediate needs, allowing students to schedule conferences with you as well. Assess which students have the greatest need for intervention or more frequent instructional support—every one to two weeks.

Planning Calendars

Planning calendars help teachers schedule and manage assessments throughout the school year. Teachers can use the masters in the Appendix to note key dates for administering and gathering assessment data for an entire class or for individual students.

Year-at-a-Glance Planning Calendar Record state, district, and classroom scheduled assessment dates. (See Appendix page 104)

Month-at-a-Glance Planning Calendar Record progress-monitoring assessments for the entire class or 1–3 students per day. (See Appendix page 105)

Week-at-a-Glance Planning Calendar Record progress-monitoring assessments and individual reading conferences for the week. (See Appendix page 106)

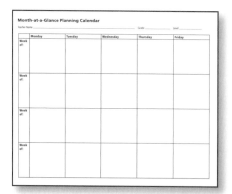
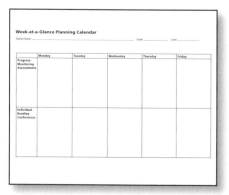

Managing Assessments

Start with one assessment tool and gradually build to the desired collection, as indicated in the following implementation steps.

1. Organize your classroom learning environment. Establish consistent routines and clear expectations for a variety of instructional settings, including whole-group, small-group, and independent activities.

2. Create a management system and schedule for administering formal and informal assessment measures. Identify a simple storage and retrieval system. Set a manageable schedule.

3. Start slowly and proceed one student at a time until all are assessed and you have identified their literacy developmental stages, strengths, and needs.

4. Create class profiles of your findings to serve as a lesson-planning reference and cumulative documentation of growth. Update the profile with each month's individual student conference data.

5. Reflect on the information gathered:

    Are students progressing in a timely fashion?

    What is their overall growth during a specified time frame?

    Are your goals for students being met?

    Is your assessment informing instruction and vice versa?

    Do you see transfer of the skills, strategies, and behaviors you have modeled and taught?

    Do the students in your class reflect the California Common Core ELA Standards and the California English Language Development Standards and expectations for their grade level?

Organizing and Storing Assessment Materials

A simple plan for collecting and retrieving each type of record will ensure success and ongoing implementation.

Color-code and use separate pocket folders or three-ring binders for each aspect of literacy to be assessed. Have a clearly identified and labeled location to house the individual student assessment folders or binders. Within each folder or binder, use dividers and pockets to store the completed individual assessment tools and work samples.

Store the completed group profile charts in lesson-planning books or create a separate three-ring binder. The binder can serve as an instructional reference tool and cumulative documentation of teaching and learning. Use index tab dividers to note the different profile charts to be collected and used over a school year. Include national, state, and district grade-level recommendations and expectations to complete this instructional reference binder.

Observations and Responsive Teaching

Daily observations of students engaged in meaningful literacy experiences provide detailed information regarding literacy and language development, strengths, and needs. Documenting observations on a regular basis provides opportunities for teachers to reflect on instruction and identify areas in need of further assessment. In their book *Integrating Differentiated Instruction and Understanding by Design: Connecting Content and Kids* (2006), Tomlinson and McTighe remind us that "Responsive teaching suggests a teacher will make modifications in how students get access to important ideas and skills, in ways that students make sense of and demonstrate essential ideas and skills, and in the learning environment—all with an eye to supporting maximum success for each learner." Observations of student learning and transfer provide the link between the assessment and instruction processes.

Anecdotal Notes

Anecdotal notes are the observations that are written by the teacher during or after a literacy event. These detailed notes capture students' processing behaviors so they may be further analyzed and used to inform the next instructional move. Anecdotal notes can be taken in whole-group or small-group settings or for individuals. These informal notes contain valuable information about students' strengths, weaknesses, progress, needs, processing abilities, or any other observations teachers feel are significant.

Use the Anecdotal Notes master (Appendix page 107) to record notes and observations. Place one small self-stick note per student in each box. After recording the student's name, date, and your observations, transfer the self-stick notes to each individual student's portfolio.

Developmental Checklists

Readers generally move through four developmental stages as they learn to read. The stages are emergent, early, transitional, and fluent. Understanding the developmental stages and their characteristics enables teachers to select appropriate materials and methodologies to support each learner. A variety of assessment tools can be used to note reading development and progress over time for individual students and small groups of learners. Additional checklists that focus on first-language reading behaviors and experiences and English-language development are provided to support the language and literacy acquisition of English learners. Use these assessment tools periodically throughout the year to record observations and notations of student growth.

Observation Checklist of First-Language Reading Behaviors and Experiences

Name _____ Date _____

Directions: Students who are new to the English language will progress in their English literacy development at different rates based on their prior first-language literacy behaviors and experiences. Use this checklist to help you identify the level of support each of your new ELs may need.

Literacy Behaviors and Experiences	Yes	No	Do Not Know
Student has attended school on a regular basis.			
Student can show how a book is read.			
Student recognizes familiar illustrations and photographs from literature.			
Student can read in his or her first language.			
Student can write in his or her first language.			
Student can find first-language cognates in English texts.			

Based on your observations, use the following suggestions to inform your instructional decisions.

If the student does not exhibit age-appropriate reading behaviors in his or her first language, you will need to provide intensive support and instruction in both English language and literacy.

If the student demonstrates age-appropriate reading behaviors in his or her first language, the student is likely to make rapid literacy progress directly correlated with English-language development.

Notes:

_____

_____

_____

Concepts About Print Assessment

Name _____ Date _____

What to Ask	What to Look For	Results	
Where is the cover?	Student points to the cover.	Yes	No
Where is the title?	Student points to the title on the cover.	Yes	No
Where is the author's name?	Student points to the author's name on the cover.	Yes	No
How should I open the book?	Student correctly demonstrates how to open the book.	Yes	No
Where is the first page?	Student points to the title page.	Yes	No
Where is the top of the page?	Student points to the title at the top of the page.	Yes	No
Where is the bottom of the page?	Student points to the author's name at the bottom of the page.	Yes	No
(Turn to a spread.) Where are some words?	Student points to any words on the page.	Yes	No
Where is a picture?	Student points to a photo or drawing on the page.	Yes	No
Where should I start reading?	Student points to the first word on the page.	Yes	No
How should my finger move as I read?	Student moves finger left to right under the line of print.	Yes	No
Can you point to the words as I read this line?	Student correctly demonstrates one-to-one matching as you read.	Yes	No
How many words are in this line?	Student correctly identifies the number of words in the line.	Yes	No
Where should I start reading next?	Student points to the first word in the second line of print.	Yes	No
Where is an uppercase letter on the page?	Student points to an uppercase letter at the beginning of any sentence.	Yes	No
Can you point to the first letter in a word?	Student points to the first letter in any word.	Yes	No
Can you point to the last letter in a word?	Student points to the last letter in any word.	Yes	No
(Point to a period on any page.) What is this punctuation mark? What does it mean?	Student says "It tells you stop because the sentence is done" or gives a similar explanation. Student says "period."	Yes	No
(Point to a question mark on any page.) What is this punctuation mark? What does it mean?	Student says "Someone is asking something" or gives a similar explanation. Student says "question mark."	Yes	No
(Point to an exclamation point on any page.) What is this punctuation mark? What does it mean?	Student says "It means you use an excited voice" or gives a similar explanation. Student says "exclamation point."	Yes	No
(Point to a comma on any page.) What is this punctuation mark? What does it mean?	Student says "It tells you to pause" or gives a similar explanation. Student says "comma."	Yes	No

Individual Reading Observation Checklists

Using a Reading Observation Checklist of observable behaviors allows teachers to focus attention on what a student understands about the reading process. The assessment measures student understanding in the areas of linking prior knowledge, reading for meaning, developing vocabulary, developing comprehension, and responding to the text.

Administration

1. Once a month, or on a regular basis, schedule time to observe each student reading independently.

2. Copy the Individual Reading Observation Checklist form for each student's stage of development or grade level.

3. On each form, record the student's name and the date.

4. Prior to the observation, read through the checklist to become familiar with the list of behaviors you may be observing while the student is reading.

5. For each criterion, determine if the student is at the beginning, progressing, or proficient stage of reading development.

6. Check the appropriate column for behaviors that are at the beginning, progressing, and proficient stages.

7. Ask the student to read aloud from the text.

8. Use the bottom of the page to record any observations or comments made during the oral reading. If needed, conduct a brief interview for additional information regarding a student's understanding of particular reading behaviors.

9. After analyzing, place the Individual Reading Observation Checklist in the appropriate organized storage location.

Using the Results

1. After completing the checklist, review the form to determine the behaviors that the student demonstrates control over in his or her reading development.

2. Determine which one or two teaching points are now most important for the student's development. Consider the areas checked off in the beginning column. Choose the teaching points based upon the student's strengths and areas of greatest need.

3. Plan to conduct a reading conference or lesson to address the areas of greatest need in an individualized setting.

Individual Reading Observation Record • Levels A/1–C/4

Name _____ Date _____ Text Title _____ Text Level _____

Reading Behavior	Beginning	Progressing	Proficient
Reads fluently; problem-solves on one or two things only			
One-to-one matching			
Directionality			
Return sweep			
Knows a small core of high-frequency words that can be read fluently			
Self-monitors and attends to print, using high-frequency words			
Aware of errors and searches the picture as well as the print			
Rereads by returning to the beginning of the sentence			
Cross-checks prediction at point of difficulty with the picture and print			
Rereads at point of difficulty and articulates the first letter of the problem word			

Comments/Concerns:

Individual Reading Observation Record • Levels D/5–E/8

Name _____ Date _____ Text Title _____ Text Level _____

Reading Behavior	Beginning	Progressing	Proficient
Reads fluently; problem-solves on one or two things only			
Returns to reread closer to the point of difficulty			
Beginning to search through a difficult word for additional information by blending letters into sounds			
Fluently uses beginning chunks, or parts of words, and ending sounds			
Meaning and structure are guiding the reading			
Integrating meaning, structure, and visual cues; is moving towards automaticity			
Self-monitoring, or checking on him or herself; moving toward automaticity			
Analyzes words using graphophonic patterns			
Reads high-frequency words fluently			
Recognizes errors when reading and initiates problem-solving actions			

Comments/Concerns:

Individual Reading Observation Record • Levels F/9–I/16

Name _____ Date _____ Text Title _____ Text Level _____

Reading Behavior	Beginning	Progressing	Proficient
Reads fluently; problem-solves on one or two things only			
Problem-solves at the point of error and makes multiple attempts to self-correct			
Searches through the difficult word and blends sounds together			
Takes words apart using large units or syllables			
Meaning and structure guide the reading; uses visual information to check on reading			
Reads longer texts with greater accuracy			
Uses word meaning and context clues to problem-solve			
Increasing control of visual patterns and flexible use of strategies			
Reads high-frequency words fluently			

Comments/Concerns:

Individual Reading Observation Record • Levels J/18–M/28

Name _____ Date _____ Text Title _____ Text Level _____

Reading Behavior	Beginning	Progressing	Proficient
Uses nonfiction text features to locate information on a topic, including table of contents, headings, glossaries, boldfaced print, indices			
Interprets and uses nonfiction text features such as maps, charts, tables, flow charts, diagrams, time lines			
Decodes text using knowledge of common letter-sound correspondences, including blends, digraphs, consonant variants, r-controlled vowels, and a variety of spelling patterns			
Decodes text using knowledge of the structure of words such as endings, prefixes, suffixes, compound words, contractions, and root words			
Identifies variant sounds of consonants and vowels			
Integrates meaning, structure, and visual cues to decode and comprehend text			
Uses strategies of sampling, predicting, confirming, and self-correction independently			
Makes inferences from texts			
Reads longer, less-predictable texts with complex text structures			
Identifies nonfiction text structures such as descriptive, problem/solution, time/order, compare/contrast, cause/effect, and directions			

Comments/Concerns:

Individual Reading Observation Checklist • Levels N/30–X/60

Name _____ Date _____ Text Title _____ Text Level _____

Competency	Beginning	Progressing	Proficient
Linking Prior Knowledge			
Relates prior experiences to the topic of the book			
Makes connections from one text to another			
Makes connections from the text to the outside world			
Reading for Meaning			
Identifies purpose for reading			
Identifies text features that will be useful			
Determines the text structure organization			
Asks questions to self when reading			
Clarifies confusing parts by rereading, defining unfamiliar words, using graphic features, and skimming			
Developing Vocabulary			
Uses knowledge of word structures (such as root words, inflectional endings, compound words, contractions, prefixes, suffixes) to determine word meaning			
Uses context clues to determine word meaning			
Identifies synonyms, antonyms, homonyms			
Understands denotation and connotation			

Individual Reading Observation Checklist • Levels N/30–X/60

Name _____ Date _____ Text Title _____ Text Level _____

Developing Comprehension	Beginning	Progressing	Proficient
Uses text features (such as table of contents, headings, captions, sidebars, glossary, index, bold print) to locate information			
Uses graphic features (such as maps, charts, tables, time lines, graphs, diagrams) to interpret information			
Summarizes or paraphrases information			
Makes predictions			
Makes inferences			
Compares and contrasts information			
Draws conclusions			
Identifies main idea and supporting details			
Identifies sequence or steps in a process			
Identifies cause and effect			
Analyzes text structure and organization (such as descriptive, comparative, sequential/time order, cause/effect, problem/solution, procedural, narrative)			
Analyzes character			
Analyzes story elements (setting, plot, theme, genre, mood, narrative point of view)			
Interprets figurative language			
Evaluates author's purpose and point of view			
Evaluates fact and opinion			
Makes judgments			
Creates graphic organizers to retell, compare and contrast, or summarize the information			
Identifies themes of the text			
Applies knowledge learned from text in various situations			
Evaluates texts for accuracy			
Draws conclusions from the texts			

Level Screener

The Level Screener is a tool that helps you maximize the time you spend with students. The tool consists of short text passages that include a standard introduction and a follow-up comprehension question. Each passage is designed to give a quick view of a student's reading level and help you determine where to begin more detailed assessment using Oral Reading Records.

Administering the Level Screener

Before you sit down with each student, select an appropriate passage. If you know a little about your students, then you may know where to begin. If not, follow this simple prescreener:

1. *Fundamental Skills*: Place a book on the table in front of the student. Ask the student to pick up the book and get ready to read. Does the student hold the book correctly and open to the first page?

2. *Letter Recognition Skills:* Write the letters **m**, **a**, **s**, and **t**. Point to each letter one at a time. Can the student name each letter?

3. *Basic Phonics Skills:* Point to each letter (from question 2) one at a time. Can the student make the sound of each letter?

If the student answers any of the above questions incorrectly, begin Oral Reading Records with a level AA text. If the student answers the questions correctly, begin with Screener: Passage 1.

The overlapping grades/ages are designed to include the typical range of students within each grade.

- Kindergarten–First Grade (page 24): Screener 1 (Level B); Comprehension Question Answer: c
- First Grade–Second Grade (page 25): Screener 2 (Level F); Comprehension Question Answer: b
- Second Grade–Third Grade (page 26): Screener 3 (Level J); Comprehension Question Answer: a
- Third Grade–Fifth Grade (page 27): Screener 4 (Level P); Comprehension Question Answer: a
- Fourth Grade–Seventh Grade (page 28): Screener 5 (Level U); Comprehension Question Answer: c

Step One: Listen to the student read the passage.

The student should not take more than 3–5 minutes to read. If the student is laboring over reading the passage, ask him or her to stop. Then give the student an easier passage to read. Remember, this is not a test. The screener is a guide for you to use as you place each student into the appropriate leveled assessment texts.

Step Two: Use the following chart to guide your decisions in the use of the Level Screener passages.

Screener Level	Reading Behaviors Observed	Next Steps
Screener: Passage 1	• Read text with no difficulty • No errors • Fluent; read text independently • Answered comprehension question accurately	Administer Screener: Passage 2 or begin Oral Reading Record assessment at level D or level E
	• Read text with minimal difficulty • One or no errors • Fluent in most places • Answered comprehension question accurately	Administer Screener: Passage 2 or begin Oral Reading Record assessment at level C
	• Read text with minimal difficulty • One or no errors • Fluent, with some exceptions • Answered comprehension question incorrectly	Begin Oral Reading Record assessment at level B
	• Read text with some difficulty • Two or three errors • Fluent in some places • Answered comprehension question accurately	Begin Oral Reading Record assessment at level B
	• Unable to read the text • More than three errors • Struggled • Answered comprehension question incorrectly or not at all	Begin Oral Reading Record assessment at level AA or administer alternative emergent literacy assessments (letter identification, word knowledge, writing)

Screener Level	Reading Behaviors Observed	Next Steps
Screener Passage 2	• Read text with no difficulty • Three or fewer errors • Fluent; read text independently • Answered comprehension question accurately	Administer Screener: Passage 3 or begin Oral Reading Record assessment at level H or level I
	• Read text with minimal difficulty • Four to five errors • Fluent in most places • Answered comprehension question accurately	Begin Oral Reading Record assessment at level H
	• Read text with minimal difficulty • Four to five errors • Fluent, with some exceptions • Answered comprehension question incorrectly	Begin Oral Reading Record assessment at level F
	• Read text with some difficulty • Six or eight errors • Fluent in some places • Answered comprehension question accurately	Begin Oral Reading Record assessment at level E
	• Unable to read the text • More than eight errors • Struggled • Answered comprehension question incorrectly or not at all	Administer Screener: Passage 1 or begin Oral Reading Record assessment at level C or level D
Screener Passage 3	• Read text with no difficulty • Two or fewer errors • Fluent; read text independently • Answered comprehension question accurately	Administer Screener: Passage 4 or begin Oral Reading Record assessment at level K or level L
	• Read text with minimal difficulty • Three to four errors • Fluent in most places • Answered comprehension question accurately	Administer Screener: Passage 4 or begin Oral Reading Record assessment at level J
(continued)	• Read text with minimal difficulty • Three to four errors • Fluent, with some exceptions • Answered comprehension question incorrectly	Begin Oral Reading Record assessment at level I

Screener Level	Reading Behaviors Observed	Next Steps
Screener Passage 3 (cont'd)	• Read text with some difficulty • Five to ten errors • Fluent in some places • Answered comprehension question accurately	Begin Oral Reading Record assessment at level H
	• Unable to read the text • More than ten errors • Struggled • Answered comprehension question incorrectly or not at all	Administer Screener: Passage 2 or begin Oral Reading Record assessment at level G
Screener Passage 4	• Read text with no difficulty • One or no errors • Fluent; read text independently • Answered comprehension question accurately	Administer Screener: Passage 5 or begin Oral Reading Record assessment at level R or level S
	• Read text with minimal difficulty • Two to three errors • Fluent in most places • Answered comprehension question accurately	Administer Screener: Passage 5 or begin Oral Reading Record assessment at level P
	• Read text with minimal difficulty • Two to three errors • Fluent, with some exceptions • Answered comprehension question incorrectly	Begin Oral Reading Record assessment at level O
	• Read text with some difficulty • Four to nine errors • Fluent in some places • Answered comprehension question accurately	Begin Oral Reading Record assessment at level N
	• Unable to read the text • More than ten errors • Struggled • Answered comprehension question incorrectly or not at all	Administer Screener: Passage 3 or begin Oral Reading Record assessment at level K or level L

Screener Level	Reading Behaviors Observed	Next Steps
Screener Passage 5	• Read text with no difficulty • One or no errors • Fluent; read text independently • Answered comprehension question accurately	Begin Oral Reading Record assessment at level V
	• Read text with minimal difficulty • Two to three errors • Fluent in most places • Answered comprehension question accurately	Begin Oral Reading Record assessment at level U
	• Read text with minimal difficulty • Two to three errors • Fluent, with some exceptions • Answered comprehension question incorrectly	Begin Oral Reading Record assessment at level T
	• Read text with some difficulty • Four to nine errors • Fluent in some places • Answered comprehension question accurately	Begin Oral Reading Record assessment at level T
	• Unable to read the text • More than ten errors • Struggled • Answered comprehension question incorrectly or not at all	Administer Screener: Passage 4 or begin Oral Reading Record assessment at level R or level S

My Dog

My dog likes to play.

My dog likes to play ball.

I like to play, too.

Choose the correct answer.

What does the dog like to do?

a. The dog likes to sleep.

b. The dog likes to eat.

c. The dog likes to play.

Ocean Living

This seal hunts and eats in very cold water.
It can sleep in cold water, too.
Fat keeps the seal alive when it can't find food.

Choose the correct answer.

What do you think seals eat?

a. Seals eat land animals.

b. Seals eat ocean animals.

c. Seals eat tall trees.

Space Monkey

In 1948 the first living animal flew into space. A monkey took off from New Mexico. There was very little news about this important event. Twenty years later, after many more animals traveled into space, men landed on the moon. The Apollo 11 moon landing took place in 1969. The flight would not have been possible had animal heroes not paved the way.

Choose the correct answer.

Why did the author write the last sentence?

a. to explain why the animal flights were important

b. to make the reader laugh

c. because the author likes animals

The Ball

On July 9, 2011, Derek Jeter stepped up to home plate for a chance to make his 3,000th hit. The bleachers were filled with New York Yankees fans as the ball cracked off Jeter's bat and headed straight for home run territory. One lucky fan snagged the ball. Although Christian Lopez could have sold that ball for hundreds of thousands of dollars, his big heart beat out any hint of greed. Lopez gave the ball back to Derek Jeter. When asked why, Lopez simply said, "Mr. Jeter deserved it."

Choose the correct answer.

Why is Christian Lopez described as a "lucky fan"?

a. He caught the ball Derek Jeter hit for his 3,000th hit.

b. He was at a baseball game.

c. He is not greedy.

from
The Story of Doctor Dolittle
by Hugh Lofting

He was very fond of animals and kept many kinds of pets. Besides the goldfish in the pond at the bottom of his garden, he had rabbits in the pantry, white mice in his piano, a squirrel in the linen closet and a hedgehog in the cellar. He had a cow with a calf too, and an old, lame horse—twenty-five years of age— and chickens, and pigeons, and two lambs, and many other animals. But his favorite pets were Dab-Dab the duck, Jip the dog, Gub-Gub the baby pig, Polynesia the parrot, and the owl Too-Too.

Choose the correct answer.
The author is describing the main character, Doctor Dolittle.
What do you know about Doctor Dolittle?
a. Doctor Dolittle was a happy man.
b. Doctor Dolittle lived on a farm.
c. Doctor Dolittle liked all kinds of animals.

Overview of Oral Reading Records

Oral Reading Records are detailed assessments that include teacher observation, recording of reading behaviors, and analysis of miscues. Oral Reading Records are administered individually in order to evaluate reading behaviors, guide instruction, check the difficulty of text, and monitor and document progress.

An Oral Reading Record allows the teacher to record observations, compare them with the text, and reflect on the strategies that students are using. The Oral Reading Record Analysis Form provides a format for recording such information as scoring results, cues used and neglected, processing behaviors and strategies, and comprehension.

Instructions for Administering, Scoring, and Analyzing Oral Reading Records

Administration

1. Make a copy of the Oral Reading Record Analysis Form (see pages 35 to 38) and the Oral Reading Record Form (see page 34) for each student.

2. Conduct an Oral Reading Record using a seen or unseen text.

Oral Reading Records allow you to observe a student without offering assistance. Only if the student has exhausted all problem-solving abilities should you give a prompt. As the student reads, use the following coding system for recording errors and miscues.

After recording the oral reading and listening to the student retell the text, analyze the observations. A close look at the student's **scoring, cues used and neglected, processing behaviors and strategies, and comprehension/ retelling check** helps you make an informed decision about the student's progress and future learning needs. Let's discuss these categories one by one.

Reading Behavior	Definition	Code
Accurate Reading	Reading without error	Place a ✓ over the word.
Substitution	Substituting an incorrect word for the correct word in the text	Draw a line over the word and write the student's word above the line: make / made
Omission	Leaving out a word or phrase	Draw a line over the word(s) and a dotted line above it: ---------- / made
Insertion	Adding a word or phrase not included in the text	Draw a line at the point of error. Write the word(s) above the line and a dotted line below it: he / ==== / he
Repetition	Repeating a word or phrase	Draw an arrow (➔) from the point of error to show how far back the student reread, whether it was a word, phrase, paragraph, or page.
Self-Correction	Correcting an error without assistance	Draw a line over the word. Write the error above the line, then add SC: make SC / made
Use of Visual Cues	Using letter and sound cues to problem-solve a word	Draw a line over the word and indicate the student's vocalizations above: m-a-d / made

Scoring

To determine the **error rate**, divide the number of words by the number of errors and round the result to the nearest whole number (X). This creates a ratio of 1:X. Next, locate the ratio on the chart below. Always go DOWN to the next lower number if the exact ratio is not shown. (For example, if your ratio is 1:16, go to 1:14 on the chart.) Finally, locate the corresponding **percent of accuracy**.

Error rate	1:100	1:50	1:35	1:25	1:20			
Accuracy Percentage	99	98	97	96	95			
Proficiency	Independent							

Error rate	1:17	1:14	1:12.5	1:11.75	1:10			
Accuracy Percentage	94	93	92	91	90			
Proficiency	Instructional							

Error rate	1:9	1:8	1:7	1:6	1:5	1:4	1:3	1:2
Accuracy Percentage	89	87.5	85.5	83	80	75	66	50
Proficiency	Frustrational							

To determine the **self-correction (SC) rate**, add together the errors and the SCs and then divide by the number of SCs to create a ratio of 1:X. In general, SC rates of 1:1–1:2 (excellent) or 1:3–1:5 (good) indicate that a student is monitoring appropriately and discovering information in the text that signals when something is wrong.

Cues Used or Neglected

Cues are simply defined as sources of information within the text. A reader constantly builds and integrates the networks of information and uses them to check and confirm responses. After the student reads, analyze each error and self-correction according to the meaning, structure, or visual cue used.

Semantic (Meaning) cues relate to the author's intended message and purpose as well as the reader's background knowledge and identification of particular concepts found within the text. Graphic features such as pictures, diagrams, and maps also help the reader gain access to the text's meaning.

Syntactic (Structural) cues are derived from the reader's oral language and exposure to book talk that allows him or her to predict upcoming text. Good readers monitor grammatical substitutions by asking, "Does it sound right this way?"

Graphophonic (Visual) cues relate to the letters, sounds, and words incorporated into a text. These elements require the reader to access the visual information in order to problem-solve.

The Oral Reading Record Analysis Form provides space in which to note and analyze cue sources used or neglected. For each error and self-correction, determine which cue source likely prompted the response by asking yourself questions such as:

Did the student use meaning to self-correct errors?
Are the student's errors meaningful? Does the reading still make sense even though the wrong word was used?
Are the student's errors grammatically correct?
Did the student use visual information in making attempts, errors, or self-corrections?

Processing Behaviors and Strategies

Next, analyze the behaviors and strategies the student uses both while reading fluently and at points of difficulty. Strategies are defined as problem-solving actions the reader employs to gain meaning from the text, such as:

- predicting future events
- anticipating language structures and patterns from text
- rereading to self-monitor
- cross-checking one cue source with another
- searching for visual patterns and elements
- self-correcting when aware of dissonance
- reading fluently and expressively
- problem-solving flexibly according to different purposes
- building on background knowledge to make sense of the text
- searching graphic features such as pictures, diagrams, maps, and tables for meaning
- using text features such as the table of contents, headings, glossary, and index to read for a purpose

The following questions can guide you in this stage of analysis:

Does the student reread to confirm meaning?
Does the student search for meaning in the pictures, diagrams, and tables?
Does the student search for visual patterns?
Does the student cross-check cue sources?
How does the student attempt unknown words?
Does the student appeal for help at points of difficulty?
Does the student wait to be told a problem word?
Are multiple cues used in self-correction?
Are various strategies used when problem-solving?
Was the text read fluently and with expression?

Comprehension/Retelling Check

To assess comprehension, ask the student to tell about the book in his or her own words. Record the response on the second page of the Oral Reading Record, and follow up with the comprehension questions. Finally, determine the student's level of understanding by analyzing his or her knowledge of the text's main idea as well as the number and type of details included in the retelling and answers.

Using the Results

1. Review the information gathered. Consider how this information will affect your instruction.

   • Are the needs of this student similar to those of others in the class?
   • Would some students benefit most from small-group or individual lessons?
   • What is the impact of your findings regarding text level difficulty?
   • Is this level a good choice for the student at this time?
   • Would some students benefit from having a more difficult or easier text?
   • Is a student showing signs of monitoring his/her reading and utilizing fix-up strategies?
   • Is the student comprehending and reading for meaning?
   • Did the student respond to the text reflectively?

2. Staple the Oral Reading Record Analysis Form on top of the Oral Reading Record Form and place it in the appropriate, organized storage location.

Oral Reading Record

Student's Name _____   Date _____

Text Title _____   Level _____

Reading Level _____   Score _____

Page #	Text	Cues used: Errors			Cues used: Self-Corrections		
		M	**S**	**V**	**M**	**S**	**V**
Totals:							

Comments:

Key to Cues
M = meaning
S = structure
V = visual

Oral Reading Record Analysis: Levels A/1–E/8

Directions: Use the prompts below to analyze the student's oral reading records.

Name _____   Date _____

School _____   Teacher _____

Text Title _____   Seen _____

Text Level _____   Unseen _____

Scoring			
Scores:	1: _ Error Rate	____% Accuracy	1: _ SC Rate	
The scores are at the:	____Independent Level	____Instructional Level	____Frustrational Level	
Cues Used and Neglected			
On errors, the student predominantly uses:	____meaning cues	____structure cues	____visual cues	
On self-corrections, the student predominantly uses:	____meaning cues	____structure cues	____visual cues	
Processing Behaviors and Strategies			
The student appears to control:	__one-to-one matching on one-syllable words	____one-to-one matching on multisyllable words	____directionality left to right	
	____directionality on return sweep	____locating known words	____locating unknown words	
At a point of difficulty, the student:	____shows flexible use of strategies	____self-corrects using different cues	____cross-checks cue sources	
	____appeals for help	____rereads to confirm	____uses pictures	
	____uses the first letter	____searches for visual patterns	____uses known words to solve unknown words	
	____waits to be told	____attempts unfamiliar words	____makes multiple attempts	
The student:	____reads word by word	____uses fluent phrasing	____uses expression	____uses punctuation
Comprehension/Retelling Check			
When retelling, the student's knowledge of the text's main idea:	____is lacking	____is teacher prompted	____is accurate	
When retelling, the student uses:	____no details	____few details	____several details	____extensive details

Oral Reading Record Analysis: Levels F/9–I/16

Directions: Use the prompts below to analyze the student's oral reading records.

Name _____ Date _____

School _____ Teacher _____

Text Title _____ Seen _____

Text Level _____ Unseen _____

Scoring			
Scores:	1:_ Error Rate	___% Accuracy	1:_ SC Rate	
The scores are at the:	___Independent Level	___Instructional Level	___Frustrational Level	
Cues Used and Neglected			
On errors, the student predominantly uses:	___meaning cues	___structure cues	___visual cues	
On self-corrections, the student predominantly uses:	___meaning cues	___structure cues	___visual cues	
Processing Behaviors and Strategies			
At a point of difficulty, the student:	___self-corrects using different cues	___uses known words to solve unknown words	___waits to be told	
	___shows flexible use of strategies	___shows increasing control of visual patterns	___attempts unfamiliar words	
	___uses word meaning and context clues to problem-solve	___problem-solves at the point of error and makes multiple attempts to self-correct	___searches through the problem word and blends sounds together	
	___cross-checks cue sources	___searches for visual patterns	___reads high-frequency words fluently	
	___appeals for help	___rereads to confirm		
The student:	___reads word by word	___uses fluent phrasing	___uses expression	___uses punctuation
Comprehension/Retelling Check			
When retelling, the student's knowledge of the text's main idea:	___is lacking	___is teacher prompted	___is accurate	
When retelling, the student uses:	___no details	___few details	___several details	___extensive details

Oral Reading Record Analysis: Levels J/18–M/28

Directions: Use the prompts below to analyze the student's oral reading records.

Name _____ Date _____

School _____ Teacher _____

Text Title _____ Seen _____

Text Level _____ Unseen _____

Scoring			
Scores:	1: _ Error Rate	____% Accuracy	1: _ SC Rate
The scores are at the:	____Independent Level	____Instructional Level	____Frustrational Level
Cues Used and Neglected			
On errors, the student predominantly uses:	____meaning cues	____structure cues	____visual cues
On self-corrections, the student predominantly uses:	____meaning cues	____structure cues	____visual cues
Processing Behaviors and Strategies			
The student:	____uses nonfiction text features (table of contents, headings, glossary, index, diagrams, etc.) to locate information and read for a purpose	____decodes text using knowledge of sound/symbol relationships, including blends, digraphs, and irregular spelling patterns	____decodes text using context clues, word structures, inflectional endings, and simple prefixes and suffixes
	____integrates meaning, structure, and visual cues to decode and comprehend text	____reads fluently, only needing to problem-solve on one or two items	____problem-solves mostly "in the head" rather than in observable ways
	____applies flexible strategies with good control of visual patterns	____builds on background knowledge to make sense of text	____reads word by word
The student:	____uses fluent phrasing	____uses expression	____uses punctuation
Comprehension/Retelling Check			
When retelling, the student's knowledge of the text's main idea:	____is lacking	____is teacher prompted	____is accurate
When retelling, the student uses:	____no details	____few details	____several details

Oral Reading Record Analysis: Levels N/30+

Name _____ Date _____

School _____ Teacher _____

Text Title _____ Seen _____

Text Level _____ Unseen _____

Level I Analysis: Scoring

Error Rate _____ Easy _____

Accuracy % _____ Instructional _____

Self-Correction Rate _____ Hard _____

Level II Analysis: Cues Used or Neglected

Check the cue(s) that are predominantly used on errors:

☐ meaning   ☐ structure   ☐ visual

Check the cue(s) that are predominantly used in self-correction:

☐ meaning   ☐ structure   ☐ visual

Level III Analysis: Processing Behaviors and Strategies

Check the processing behaviors and strategies that are used:

☐ uses nonfiction text features (table of contents, headings, glossary, index, diagrams, etc.) to locate information and to read for a purpose

☐ decodes text using knowledge of sound/symbol relationships, including blends, digraphs, and irregular spelling patterns

☐ decodes text using context clues, word structures, inflectional endings, and simple prefixes and suffixes

☐ integrates meaning, structure, and visual cues to decode and comprehend text

☐ builds on background knowledge to make sense of text

☐ applies flexible strategies with good control of visual patterns

☐ reads fluently, problem-solving on one or two things only

☐ most problem-solving on text is done in the student's head and is not observable

Fluency   ☐ word by word   ☐ fluent phrasing   ☐ uses expression   ☐ uses punctuation

Level IV Analysis: Comprehension/Retelling Check

Knowledge of Main Idea			Use of Detail			
No	Teacher Prompted	Yes	None	Few	Several	Extensive

Assessing Reading Phrasing/Fluency, Intonation, Pace, and Accuracy

Name _____   Date _____

Reading phrasing/fluency, intonation, pace, and accuracy may be assessed any time a student reads aloud. Discuss the assessment rubric, modeling each description, so students know what you expect.

Rating Scale	PHRASING/FLUENCY
1	Reads word by word. Does not attend to author's syntax or sentence structures. Has limited sense of phrase boundaries.
2	Reads slowly and in a choppy manner, usually in two-word phrases. Some attention is given to author's syntax and sentence structures.
3	Reads in phrases of three to four words. Appropriate syntax is used.
4	Reads in longer, more meaningful phrases. Regularly uses pitch, stress, and author's syntax to reflect comprehension.
	INTONATION
1	Reads in a monotone and does not attend to punctuation.
2	Reads with some intonation and some attention to punctuation. Reads in a monotone at times.
3	Reads by adjusting intonation appropriately. Consistently attends to punctuation.
4	Reads with intonation that reflects feeling, anticipation, tension, and mood.
	PACE
1	Slow and laborious reading.
2	Reading is either moderately slow or inappropriately fast.
3	Unbalanced combination of slow and fast reading.
4	Reading is consistently natural, conversational, and appropriate, resembling natural oral language.
	ACCURACY
1	Exhibits multiple attempts at decoding words without success. Word reading accuracy is inadequate/poor, below 85%.
2	Attempts to self-correct errors are usually unsuccessful. Word reading accuracy is marginal, between 86–90%.
3	Attempts to self-correct errors are successful. Word reading accuracy is good, between 91–95%.
4	Most words are read correctly on initial attempt. Exhibits minimal self-corrections, all successful. Word reading accuracy is excellent—96% and above.

Small-Group Reading Observation Records

Small-group lessons allow teachers to focus instruction on the strengths and needs of selected students. Observations made during small-group instruction aid in the selection of group members and potential teaching points. Observations also allow the teacher to note student growth and development. This assessment measures the reading behaviors observed during a small-group reading lesson. Teachers can use this assessment periodically to note behaviors observed in an instructional setting.

Administration

1. Make a copy of the Small-Group Reading Observation Record.

2. Fill in the group members' names, the date, text title, and level.

3. After conducting a small-group reading lesson, fill in your observations of students' reading behaviors, teacher prompting, and the validation or activation of teaching points.

Using the Results

1. Review the notes recorded on the completed Small-Group Reading Observation Records.

2. Determine the one or two most important reading behaviors or strategies students in this group need as the focus for instruction. Identify any trends or patterns for teaching points to be addressed at the whole-group level.

3. Consider the membership of your small-group reading groups. Is it time to move students to other groups for maximum instructional effectiveness?

4. Place the Small-Group Reading Observation Records in the appropriate organized storage location. Keeping cumulative records provides a useful reference for future instruction.

Small-Group Reading Observation Record

Group Members _____ Date _____

Text Title _____ Level _____

Check one:

Before Reading _____   During Reading _____   After Reading _____

Teacher Prompt: Students' Behavior:

Comments:

Focus for next small-group reading lesson:

Small-Group Reading Observation Records

The Small-Group Guided Reading Observation Records serves as a quick reference check for classroom teachers. When complete, it provides an overview of the group's reading abilities and points to areas that may need to be addressed in future lessons.

Administration

1. Once a month, collect and analyze the Individual Reading Observation Checklists you have completed for each student in your class.

2. Make one copy of the Small-Group Reading Observation Checklist sheet.

3. Record the date of the checklist analysis at the top of the Small-Group Reading Observation Checklist sheet.

4. After analyzing each individual checklist, transfer the information you learned about each student to the Small-Group Reading Observation Checklist sheet.

5. Record the stage of development for each student and each criterion. Place an asterisk (*) for behaviors that are at the proficient stage, a check mark (√) for progressing, and an "X" for beginning.

Using the Results

1. After completing your Small-Group Reading Observation Checklist chart, begin your analysis for growth and development, lesson planning, and intervention lessons.

2. Look for trends, patterns, and information that stand out.

3. Identify the areas you marked with a check mark or "X." These are the behaviors you will want to use as the focus for whole-group, small-group, or individual lessons.

4. Consider the number of students exhibiting the same stage of development for a particular behavior. If the majority of students are at the progressing stage, you may want to focus a small-group lesson for those students at the beginning stage.

5. If you notice a behavior that is at the beginning stage of development for most of your class, this can become the focus of your whole-group lessons. Remember to model the behavior for your students first, then allow them the opportunity to participate with you in a shared-reading lesson, and finally reinforce the behavior in a small-group reading lesson, or an individual lesson if needed.

6. The behaviors that stand out as individual concerns may be addressed in small-group or individualized lessons.

7. After analyzing, place Individual Reading Checklists and your Small-Group Reading Observation Checklist in the appropriate organized storage location.

Small-Group Reading Observation Record • Levels A/1–C/4

Date _____

Text Title _____

Text Level _____

Chart Coding Legend:
✓ reading behavior observed during lesson

Student's Name	Reads fluently; problem-solves on one or two things only	One-to-one matching	Directionality	Return sweep	Knows a small core of high-frequency words that can be read fluently	Self-monitors and attends to print, using high-frequency words	Aware of errors and searches the picture as well as the print	Rereads by returning to the beginning of the sentence	Cross-checks prediction at point of difficulty with the picture and print	Rereads at point of difficulty and articulates the first letter of the problem word

Comments/Concerns:

_____

_____

_____

_____

_____

_____

Small-Group Reading Observation Record • Levels D/5–E/8

Date _____

Text Title _____

Text Level _____

Chart Coding Legend:
✓ reading behavior observed during lesson

Student's Name	Reads fluently; problem-solves on one or two things only	Returns to reread closer to the point of difficulty	Beginning to search through a difficult word for additional information by blending letters into sounds	Fluently uses beginning chunks, or parts of words, and ending sounds	Meaning and structure are guiding the reading	Is integrating meaning, structure, and visual cues; is moving towards automaticity	Is self-monitoring, or checking on him or herself; moving toward automaticity	Analyzes words using graphophonic patterns	Reads high-frequency words fluently	Recognizes errors when reading and initiates problem-solving actions

Comments/Concerns:

_____

_____

_____

_____

_____

_____

_____

Small-Group Reading Observation Record • Levels F/9–I/16

Date _____

Text Title _____

Text Level _____

Chart Coding Legend:
✓ reading behavior observed during lesson

Student's Name	Reads fluently; problem-solves on one or two things only	Problem-solves at the point of error and makes multiple attempts to self-correct	Searches through the difficult word and blends sounds together	Takes words apart using large units or syllables	Meaning and structure guide the reading; uses visual information to check on reading	Reads longer texts with greater accuracy	Uses word meaning and context clues to problem-solve	Shows increasing control of visual patterns and flexible use of strategies	Reads high-frequency words fluently

Comments/Concerns:

_____

_____

_____

_____

_____

_____

_____

Small-Group Reading Observation Record • Levels J/18–M/28

Date _____

Reading Behaviors	Student Names								Comments/Concerns
• Uses nonfiction text features to locate information on a topic, including table of contents, headings, glossaries, boldfaced print, indices									
• Interprets and uses nonfiction text features such as maps, charts, tables, flow charts, diagrams, time lines									
• Decodes text using knowledge of common letter-sound correspondences, including blends, digraphs, consonant variants, r-controlled vowels, and a variety of spelling patterns									
• Decodes text using knowledge of the structure of words such as endings, prefixes, suffixes, compound words, contractions, and root words									
• Identifies variant sounds of consonants and vowels									
• Integrates meaning, structure, and visual cues to decode and comprehend text									
• Uses strategies of sampling, predicting, confirming, and self-correction independently									
• Makes inferences from texts									
• Reads longer, less-predictable texts with complex text structures									
• Identifies nonfiction text structures such as descriptive, problem/solution, time/order, compare/contrast, cause/effect, and directions									

Small-Group Reading Observation Checklist Levels N/30–X/60

Date _____

Grade _____

Student Names									Comments/ Concerns
Linking Prior Knowledge									
• Relates prior experiences to the topic of the book									
• Makes connections from one text to another									
• Makes connections from the text to the outside world									
Reading for Meaning									
• Identifies purpose for reading									
• Identifies text features that will be useful									
• Determines the text structure organization									
• Asks questions to self when reading									
• Clarifies confusing parts by rereading, defining unfamiliar words, using graphic features, and skimming									
Developing Vocabulary									
• Uses knowledge of word structures (such as root words, inflectional endings, compound words, contractions, prefixes, suffixes) to determine word meaning									
• Uses context clues to determine word meaning									
• Identifies synonyms, antonyms, homonyms									
• Understands denotation and connotation									

Small-Group Reading Observation Checklist Levels N/30–X/60

Date _____

Grade _____

	Student Names								Comments/ Concerns
Developing Comprehension									
• Uses text features (such as table of contents, headings, captions, sidebars, glossary, index, bold print) to locate information									
• Uses graphic features (such as maps, charts, tables, time lines, graphs, diagrams) to interpret information									
• Summarizes or paraphrases information									
• Makes predictions									
• Makes inferences									
• Compares and contrasts information									
• Draws conclusions									
• Identifies main idea and supporting details									
• Identifies sequence or steps in a process									
• Identifies cause and effect									
• Analyzes text structure and organization (such as descriptive, comparative, sequential/time order, cause/effect, problem/solution, procedural, narrative)									
• Analyzes character									
• Analyzes story elements (setting, plot, theme, genre, mood, narrative point of view)									
• Interprets figurative language									
• Evaluates author's purpose and point of view									
• Evaluates fact and opinion									
• Makes judgments									
Responding to the Text									
• Creates graphic organizers to retell, compare and contrast, or summarize the information									
• Identifies themes of the text									
• Applies knowledge learned from text in various situations									
• Evaluates texts for accuracy									
• Draws conclusions from the texts									

Reading Retelling Assessments and Rubrics (Oral and Written)

Both oral and written individual reading retelling rubrics provide valuable insights about students' reading comprehension and how they go about organizing concepts, ideas, and vocabulary into their own retellings. Seven retelling rubrics—narrative, cause/effect, compare/contrast, sequential/time order, procedural, descriptive, problem/solution—represent the variety of text structures found in Benchmark Education Company texts. Both narrative and expository text are included for use. The instructions for all forms are identical.

After individual assessments are completed, a Group Reading Retelling Chart may be used to create a class or group profile.

Administration

1. Decide which aspect of a student's comprehension you wish to assess and how you want to assess the student (oral or written form). For example, if you want to find out how well a student can identify problems and solutions, choose a chapter book that includes the pattern of problem/solution in the organization of the text. Before meeting with the student, make a copy of the retelling rubric that matches your chosen text structure.

2. Ask the student to read the text silently. If on a previous occasion the student has performed poorly on a retelling while reading silently, you might ask the student to read the text aloud to see if this improves comprehension.

3. Prompt the student to retell in either oral or written form what was read. (Students retell in written form on their own paper.) Allow the student to freely retell what he or she remembers from the text. It may be useful to record some anecdotal notes about the student's performance afterward. Note specific details and vocabulary that the student used.

4. If needed, prompt the student to provide more information. Ask specific questions and allow the student to refer back to the text, if needed. Some helpful questions might include:

   - *Can you tell me more about _____?*
   - *What message do you think the author wanted to convey?*
   - *What happened after _____?*
   - *What information did the tables or diagrams give you?*
   - *What was the problem?*
   - *What were the solutions that were posed?*
   - *Do you have any personal experiences that relate to this topic?*
   - *What effect did the problem have on the event or happening?*
   - *What ideas or events was the author comparing?*
   - *Can you tell me more about the characters?*

5. Take some anecdotal notes on how the student responded to your questions. Also note whether the student referred to the text to locate an answer.

6. Use the assessment form to rate the student's performance. Place a check mark in the aided or unaided column to note if the student's retelling required prompting. Circle the rubric score.

7. Total and score the rubric as a whole.

8. Record results on a Group Reading Retelling Chart to create a group or class profile.

Using the Results

1. Review the individual rubrics to gain information for future instruction.

2. Identify the areas in which the student is in need of explicit instruction. Observe the same skill on a different text. This in-depth analysis also provides the necessary information for grouping students for specific kinds of instruction.

3. Review the Group Reading Retelling Charts, and identify the text structures needing additional attention at the whole-group, small-group, and independent levels.

Nonfiction Retelling Assessment

Directions: Use the following checklist during small-group reading to evaluate students' skill in retelling information from **nonfiction** texts. Record students' names in the first column. Then record specific observations and/or mark **+** for **information given with prompts**, ✓ for **information given without prompts**, and **?** for **information not given**.

Student's Name	Explains the Topic	Provides Details to Support the Topic	Provides Details in Appropriate Sequence	Utilizes Appropriate Text Structures, such as Compare/ Contrast or Cause/Effect	Explains How the Topic Has Personal Relevance

Fiction Retelling Assessment

Directions: Use the following checklist during small-group reading to evaluate students' skill in retelling information from **fiction** texts. Record students' names in the first column. Then record specific observations and/or mark **+** for **information given with prompts**, ✓ for **information given without prompts**, and **?** for **information not given**.

Student's Name	Identifies the Genre	Names the Main Characters in the Story	Identifies the Story's Setting	Describes Plot Details in Sequential Order, Including the Beginning, Middle, and End	Explains How the Story Has Personal Relevance

Individual Reading Retelling Rubric: Descriptive Text Structure

Name _____ Date _____

Text Title _____ Level _____

Circle one: Oral Retelling   Written Retelling

Prompt: Tell me about what you read.

Rubric

4 Gives accurate information using explicit details with elaboration

3 Gives accurate information with explicit details

2 Gives limited information; may include some inaccuracies

1 Unable to give information related to the text

0 No score indicates no response

	Unaided	Aided	Rubric Score
• Retells story in appropriate sequence			1 2 3 4
• Describes the setting			1 2 3 4
• Provides details about the characters			1 2 3 4
• States the problem and solution of the story			1 2 3 4
• Provides details to support the events in the story			1 2 3 4
• Describes the ending of the story			1 2 3 4
• Explains how the story has personal relevance			1 2 3 4
• Makes connection from the story to other texts			1 2 3 4
Comments:	**Total Rubric Score**		

Individual Reading Retelling Rubric: Narrative Text Structure

Name _____ Date _____

Text Title _____ Level _____

Circle one: **Oral Retelling**   **Written Retelling**

Prompt: Tell me about what you read.

Rubric

4 Gives accurate information using explicit details with elaboration

3 Gives accurate information with explicit details

2 Gives limited information; may include some inaccuracies

1 Unable to give information related to the text

0 No score indicates no response

	Unaided	Aided	Rubric Score			
• States author's intended purpose			1	2	3	4
• Understands and explains key concepts			1	2	3	4
• Provides supportive details for key concepts			1	2	3	4
• Uses descriptive language to help the reader or listener form mind pictures			1	2	3	4
• States setting for information			1	2	3	4
• Provides details in a logical sequence			1	2	3	4
• Demonstrates an understanding of diagrams, tables, or graphs encountered in the text			1	2	3	4
• Provides a summary of the concept and how it has personal relevance			1	2	3	4
Comments:		Total Rubric Score				

Individual Reading Retelling Rubric: Problem/Solution Text Structure

Name _____   Date _____

Text Title _____   Level _____

Circle one: Oral Retelling   Written Retelling

Prompt: Tell me about what you read.

Rubric

4 Gives accurate information using explicit details with elaboration

3 Gives accurate information with explicit details

2 Gives limited information; may include some inaccuracies

1 Unable to give information related to the text ,

0 No score indicates no response

	Unaided	Aided	Rubric Score
• States author's intended purpose			1 2 3 4
• States and understands the importance of the concept			1 2 3 4
• States the problem clearly and why it happens			1 2 3 4
• Provides details about the cause of the problem			1 2 3 4
• Provides details that state the effects of the problem			1 2 3 4
• Clearly links causes and effects			1 2 3 4
• Provides a realistic solution to the problem			1 2 3 4
• Demonstrates an understanding of diagrams, tables, or graphs encountered in the text			1 2 3 4
• Provides a summary of the concept and how it has personal relevance			1 2 3 4
Comments:		**Total Rubric Score**	

Individual Reading Retelling Rubric: Sequential/Time Order Text Structure

Name _____ Date _____

Text Title _____ Level _____

Circle one: **Oral Retelling**   **Written Retelling**

Prompt: Tell me about what you read.

Rubric

4 Gives accurate information using explicit details with elaboration

3 Gives accurate information with explicit details

2 Gives limited information; may include some inaccuracies

1 Unable to give information related to the text

0 No score indicates no response

	Unaided	Aided	Rubric Score
• States author's intended purpose			1 2 3 4
• Retells events in chronological order or logical sequence			1 2 3 4
• Provides details to support the key concepts			1 2 3 4
• Demonstrates an understanding of diagrams, tables, or graphs encountered in the text			1 2 3 4
• Provides a summary of the concept and how it has personal relevance			1 2 3 4
Comments:		**Total Rubric Score**	

Individual Reading Retelling Rubric: Procedural Text Structure

Name _____ Date _____

Text Title _____ Level _____

Circle one: **Oral Retelling** **Written Retelling**

Prompt: Tell me about what you read.

Rubric

4 Gives accurate information using explicit details with elaboration

3 Gives accurate information with explicit details

2 Gives limited information; may include some inaccuracies

1 Unable to give information related to the text

0 No score indicates no response

	Unaided	Aided	Rubric Score
• States author's intended purpose			1 2 3 4
• Includes material, equipment, or ingredients needed			1 2 3 4
• Retells a detailed step-by-step sequence of how and when to do something in order to accomplish a task			1 2 3 4
• Demonstrates an understanding of diagrams, tables, or graphs encountered in the text			1 2 3 4
• Provides a summary of the concept or task and how it has personal relevance			1 2 3 4
Comments:		**Total Rubric Score**	

Individual Reading Retelling Rubric:
Compare/Contrast Text Structure

Name _____ Date _____

Text Title _____ Level _____

Circle one: **Oral Retelling** **Written Retelling**

Prompt: Tell me about what you read.

Rubric

4 Gives accurate information using explicit details with elaboration

3 Gives accurate information with explicit details

2 Gives limited information; may include some inaccuracies

1 Unable to give information related to the text

0 No score indicates no response

	Unaided	**Aided**	**Rubric Score**
• States author's intended purpose			1 2 3 4
• Understands and explains the key concepts			1 2 3 4
• Clearly compares the topic by providing at least two similarities and at least two differences			1 2 3 4
• Demonstrates an understanding of diagrams, tables, or graphs encountered in the text			1 2 3 4
• Provides a summary of the concept and how it has personal relevance			1 2 3 4
Comments:		**Total Rubric Score**	

Individual Reading Retelling Rubric: Cause/Effect Text Structure

Name _____ Date _____

Text Title _____ Level _____

Circle one: **Oral Retelling**   **Written Retelling**

Prompt: Tell me about what you read.

Rubric

4 Gives accurate information using explicit details with elaboration

3 Gives accurate information with explicit details

2 Gives limited information; may include some inaccuracies

1 Unable to give information related to the text

0 No score indicates no response

	Unaided	**Aided**	**Rubric Score**
• States author's intended purpose			1 2 3 4
• States and understands the importance of the concept			1 2 3 4
• States the event or happening			1 2 3 4
• Provides details about the cause of the event			1 2 3 4
• Provides details about the effect of the happening or event			1 2 3 4
• Clearly links causes and effects			1 2 3 4
• Demonstrates an understanding of diagrams, tables, or graphs encountered in the text			1 2 3 4
• Provides a summary of the concept and how it has personal relevance			1 2 3 4
Comments:		**Total Rubric Score**	

Individual Writing Assessment: Descriptive Frames

Name _____   Date _____

Title _____

• What is the main idea?

• What are the attributes of the main idea?

• What is the function of each attribute?

Individual Writing Assessment: Problem/Solution Frames

Name _____   Date _____

Title _____

• What is the problem?

• Who or what has the problem?

• What is causing the problem?

• What are the immediate effects of the problem?

• What are the long-lasting effects of the problem?

• Who is trying to solve the problem?

• What solutions are being tried?

• What are the obstacles to the solutions?

• What are the result of the attempted solutions?

• How is the problem resolved?

Informal Assessments—Grades K–6

Individual Writing Assessment: Sequential/Time Order Frames

Name _____ Date _____

Title _____

- What is the beginning event?

- What happened next?

- What happened after that?

- How are the events related?

- What is the final outcome?

Individual Writing Assessment: Procedural Frames

Name _____ Date _____

Title _____

• What is the procedure or event?

• What are the steps?

• How do the steps relate to each other?

• What is the end result?

Individual Writing Assessment: Compare/Contrast Frames

Name _____ Date _____

Title _____

- Describe what is being compared and contrasted.

- What attributes are being used to compare and contrast?

- What makes the objects similar?

- What makes the objects different?

Individual Writing Assessment: Cause/Effect Frames

Name _____ Date _____

Title _____

- What happens?

- What causes the event to happen?

- What are the effects of the event?

Individual Writing Assignment: Narrative Frames

Name _____ Date _____

Title _____

Beginning

Setting: **Where** does the story take place?

When does the story take place?

Who is the main character?

Problem: **What** is the problem?

Middle **What** are the events in the story that make an attempt to solve the problem?

End

Resolution: **How** is the problem solved?

Reactions: **How** do the characters feel about the resolution?

Theme: **What** is the overall moral or theme of the story?

Benchmark Advance includes opportunities for students to engage in short writing and extended writing activities with every unit and every week of instruction.

Use the **Assessment Checklists for Grades K and 1** to document students' writing progress throughout the year. These checklists help you document students' development of key foundational skills and strategies that support the writing process:

- Concepts about print

- Grammar, language, and conventions

- Spelling/sound correspondence

- Sight word recognition

- Author's craft

The checklists also track beginning and emerging writers' development in the areas of narrative, informational, and opinion writing.

For students in Grades 2–6, grade-specific **opinion, informative/explanatory, and narrative writing rubrics** help you assess students' progress in writing effectively to one or more sources. Student writing checklists aligned to the rubric expectations provide students with a tool for planning, drafting, editing, and revising their work. In addition, **writing frames** (pages 60-66) enable you to assess students' comprehension and written analysis of texts reflecting different nonfiction and narrative text structures.

Kindergarten Developmental Writing Checklist

Name _____

Directions: Use this checklist to document students' writing progress throughout the year. It is recommended that you assess students at the beginning and at the end of each school year to identify behaviors, skills, and strategies you should support or validate during independent writing and conferring time or during small-group intervention.

Behaviors, Strategies, and Skills to Observe and Support	Date	Date	Date	Date	Date
Stages of Writing Development					
Scribble stage					
Isolated letter stage					
Transitional stage					
Stylized sentence stage					
Writing stage					
Fluent stage					
Stages of Spelling Development					
Pre-phonetic: scribble writing					
Pre-phonetic: symbols					
Pre-phonetic: random letters					
Semi-phonetic: initial consonants					
Semi-phonetic: initial/final consonants					
Semi-phonetic: vowels/consonants combination in CVC words with inconsistent correct vowels (put, pot)					
Semi-phonetic: vowels/consonants combination in CVC words with correct use of vowels					
Transitional					
Correct stage					
Concepts About Print/Print Conventions					
Print carries meaning					
Beginning of text					
One-to-one correspondence					
Spaces between words					
Directionality					
Uppercase letter at beginning of sentence					
Punctuation at the end of sentence					
Rereads from beginning of sentence					

Kindergarten Developmental Writing Checklist (continued)

Behaviors, Strategies, and Skills to Observe and Support	Date	Date	Date	Date	Date
Composing/Writing Fluency					
Generates topics with teacher or peer support					
Holds the message in memory while writing					
Rereads to remember the next word in the message					
Writes a simple message of one to three sentences					
Transcribing/Encoding					
Says words slowly to listen for sounds					
Hears and records sounds in words					
Attends to letter formation					
Language and Grammar					
Uses complete sentences in oral conversation					
Writes a complete sentence					
Capitalizes "I" within a sentence					
Uses accurate adjectives					
Orally composes complete sentences with compound subjects that include the pronoun "I"					
Writes complete sentences with compound subjects that include the pronoun "I"					
Journal Writing					
Draws what he/she visualizes					
Tells about life events					
Tells thoughts and feelings					
Book Review Writing					
Includes title					
Includes author					
States opinion about characters, events, or illustrations					
Supports the opinion					
Gives a recommendation					
Informational Report Writing					
Identifies the topic					
Writes topic sentence that states main idea					
Includes two or more facts from text					

Notes:

Grade 1 Developmental Writing Checklist

Name _____

Directions: Use this checklist to document students' writing progress throughout the year. It is recommended that you assess students at the beginning and at the end of each school year to identify behaviors, skills, and strategies you should support or validate during independent writing and conferring time or during small-group intervention.

Behaviors, Strategies, and Skills to Observe and Support	Date	Date	Date	Date	Date
Stages of Writing Development					
Scribble stage					
Isolated letter stage					
Transitional stage					
Stylized sentence stage					
Writing stage					
Fluent stage					
Stages of Spelling Development					
Pre-phonetic: scribble writing					
Pre-phonetic: symbols					
Pre-phonetic: random letters					
Semi-phonetic: initial consonants					
Semi-phonetic: initial/final consonants					
Semi-phonetic: vowels/consonants combination in CVC words with inconsistent correct vowels (put, pot)					
Semi-phonetic: vowels/consonants combination in CVC words with correct use of vowels					
Transitional					
Correct stage					
Concepts About Print/Print Conventions					
Print carries meaning					
Beginning of text					
One-to-one correspondence					
Spaces between words					
Directionality					
Uppercase letter at beginning of sentence					
Punctuation at the end of sentence					
Rereads from beginning of sentence					
Book titles underlined					
Composing/Writing Fluency					
Generates topics with teacher or peer support					
Holds the message in memory while writing					
Rereads to remember the next word in the message					
Writes a simple message of one to three sentences					
Avoids overused words					
Demonstrates writer's voice					
Varies sentence beginnings					
Spells several one-syllable and high-frequency words correctly					

Grade 1 Developmental Writing Checklist (continued)

Behaviors, Strategies, and Skills to Observe and Support	Date	Date	Date	Date	Date
Transcribing/Encoding					
Says words slowly to listen for sounds					
Hears and records sounds in words					
Attends to letter formation					
Language and Grammar					
Uses complete sentences in oral conversation					
Writes a complete sentence					
Capitalizes "I" and people's names within a sentence					
Uses accurate adjectives					
Orally composes complete sentences with compound subjects that include the pronoun "I"					
Writes complete sentences with compound subjects that include the pronoun "I"					
Uses personal pronouns after naming a person, group, or object					
Journal Writing					
Draws what he/she visualizes					
Tells about life events					
Tells thoughts and feelings					
Personal Narratives					
Includes self as main character					
Includes other characters					
Describes the setting					
Includes a beginning, middle, and end					
Includes a problem in the narrative					
Develops a resolution to the problem					
Informational Report Writing					
Identifies the topic					
Writes topic sentence that states main idea					
Includes two or more facts from text					
Chooses a title that reflects the topic					
Cites sources					
Book Review Writing					
Includes title					
Includes author					
States opinion about characters, events, or illustrations					
Supports the opinion					
Gives a recommendation					

Notes:

The Developmental Stages of Writing

Scribble Stage: A student operating in the scribble stage writes with lines, scribbles, or mock-letter forms. He or she has no specific concept of the use of space on the page.

Isolated Letter Stage: During the isolated letter stage, letter forms begin to appear. Random letters and numbers recur throughout the writing sample, based on the student's developing knowledge. The student is still confused about such early concepts as words, directionality, and the use of space.

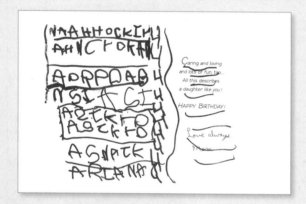

Transitional Stage: Some letter-sound correspondences and correctly spelled words begin to appear as the student moves into the transitional stage. However, they may be mixed with isolated letters and numerals.

Stylized Sentence Stage: As a student acquires a core writing vocabulary of frequently used words, he or she begins to use these words to construct sentences with simple patterns. The student is also beginning to refine concepts of spacing and letter-sound correspondence.

Writing Stage: A student moves beyond the stylized sentence stage as he or she learns to compose stories and acquires a larger writing vocabulary. The student uses more conventional spelling, longer sentences, and punctuation.

Fluent Stage: Fluent writers begin to develop strategies for the craft of writing. These strategies include elaborating (voice), critiquing their own writing and others' writing, writing in different genres, using what they know about reading text to write, using the writing process, and developing a sense of audience. Fluent writers spell most words correctly and carefully edit their spelling while they write. They also have a wide vocabulary and know how to use a thesaurus and dictionary to expand their current vocabulary. Fluent writers understand text structures (compare and contrast, descriptive, procedural, problem/solution, and cause/effect), text functions (narrative, expressive, informative, and poetic), and tenses. They write on a wide variety of topics including personal experiences and nonfiction topics.

Opinion Rubric: Grade 2

Score	Planning and Implementation	Evidence of Genre Characteristics	Conventions of Grammar and Usage	Conventions of Mechanics
4	The writer's ideas are well organized and well developed. The writer: • creates and maintains a meaningful organizational structure. • clearly maintains the opinion throughout the text. • uses well-chosen words and phrases that add effect to the opinion piece.	The writer demonstrates complete understanding of the features of an opinion text. The writer: • clearly introduces the topic. • states an opinion about the topic. • includes at least one reason for the opinion based on inferences made about the topic. • includes purposefully chosen evidence that supports the reason(s). • uses a wide variety of linking words and phrases that connect reasons with evidence. • includes an effective concluding sentence or paragraph that makes the reader think about the writer's ideas. • consistently uses third person and present tense.	The writer correctly implements all conventions of grammar and sentence structure. The writer: • writes engaging and meaningful complete and compound sentences. • uses parts of speech in unique ways. • uses grammar conventions in clear and concise ways.	The writer correctly implements all conventions of mechanics (spelling, capitalization, punctuation). The writer: • always correctly indents paragraphs. • makes no, or few, mechanical mistakes, and any mistakes do not hinder overall meaning.
3	The writer's ideas are adequately organized and developed. The writer: • creates and maintains an organizational structure. • maintains the opinion throughout the text. • uses words and phrases that add effect to the opinion piece.	The writer demonstrates an adequate understanding of the features of an opinion text. The writer: • introduces the topic. • states an opinion about the topic. • includes one reason for the opinion based on inferences made about the topic. • includes evidence that supports the reason. • uses linking words and phrases that connect reasons with evidence. • includes a concluding sentence or paragraph. • uses third person and present tense most of the time.	The writer implements most conventions of grammar and sentence structure. The writer: • writes adequate complete and compound sentences. • uses parts of speech correctly. • uses grammar conventions correctly.	The writer implements most conventions of mechanics (spelling, capitalization, punctuation). The writer: • correctly indents paragraphs most of the time. • makes occasional mechanical mistakes, but they do not hinder overall meaning.
2	The writer's ideas are somewhat organized and developed. The writer: • attempts to create an organizational structure. Ideas are difficult to follow. • inadequately maintains the opinion throughout the text. Text suggests the writer does not understand the stated opinion. • uses few words and phrases that add effect to the opinion piece.	The writer demonstrates some understanding of the features of an opinion text. The writer: • attempts to introduce the topic. • states a weak opinion about the topic. • includes a weak reason for the opinion. • includes some evidence that supports the reason, but evidence is weak. • uses some linking words and phrases that connect reasons with evidence. • includes a weak concluding sentence or paragraph. • uses third person and present tense some of the time.	The writer implements some conventions of grammar and sentence structure. The writer: • attempts to write complete and compound sentences. • uses some parts of speech correctly. • uses some grammar conventions correctly.	The writer implements some conventions of mechanics (spelling, capitalization, punctuation). The writer: • indents paragraphs some of the time. • makes many mechanical mistakes, and they hinder overall meaning.
1	The writer's ideas are disorganized and undeveloped. The writer: • does not attempt to create an organizational structure. • does not maintain the opinion throughout the text. • uses few, if any, words and phrases that add effect to the opinion piece.	The writer demonstrates little, if any, understanding of the features of an opinion text. The writer: • does not introduce the topic. • states an unclear opinion. • includes a reason for the opinion. The reason may or may not be connected to the topic. • includes little, if any, evidence that supports the reason. • uses few, if any, linking words and phrases that connect reasons with evidence. • does not include a concluding sentence or paragraph. • rarely uses third person and present tense correctly.	The writer implements few, if any, conventions of grammar and sentence structure. The writer: • does not write coherent complete and compound sentences. • rarely uses parts of speech correctly. • rarely uses grammar conventions correctly.	The writer implements few, if any, conventions of mechanics (spelling, capitalization, punctuation). The writer: • does not attempt to indent paragraphs. • makes many mechanical mistakes, and they hinder overall meaning.

Opinion Checklist: Grade 2

Name _____ Date _____

Title _____

	Yes	No	Not Sure
1. I introduce my topic.	—	—	—
2. I state my opinion at the beginning of my paper.	—	—	—
3. I include a reason for my opinion based on my own thoughts about the topic.	—	—	—
4. I use evidence to support my opinion.	—	—	—
5. I use linking words and phrases to connect reasons and evidence.	—	—	—
6. I include a concluding sentence or paragraph that makes my readers think.	—	—	—
7. My opinion follows an organized structure.	—	—	—
8. I choose words that make sense and make my opinion interesting.	—	—	—
9. I do not change my opinion.	—	—	—
10. I use different types of sentences.	—	—	—
11. I use third person and present tense.	—	—	—

Quality Writing Checklist
I looked for and corrected . . .

	Yes	No	Not Sure
parts of speech (nouns, pronouns, verbs, adjectives, adverbs).	—	—	—
grammar.	—	—	—
indented paragraphs.	—	—	—
punctuation.	—	—	—
capitalization.	—	—	—
spelling.	—	—	—

Informative/Explanatory Report Rubric: Grade 2

Score	Planning and Implementation	Evidence of Genre Characteristics	Conventions of Grammar and Usage	Conventions of Mechanics
4	The writer's ideas are well organized and well developed. The writer: • includes an introduction, or lead, that grabs readers' attention. • creates and maintains a meaningful organizational structure. • uses well-chosen words and phrases that add effect and description to the informational piece. • includes a strong conclusion that keeps readers thinking.	The writer demonstrates complete understanding of the features of an informational report. The writer: • thoroughly develops the topic by including accurate information (facts, definitions, details). • includes unique graphics that support the information. • includes thoughtfully worded captions that explain each graphic feature. • includes one or more different viewpoints so readers can draw their own conclusions. • includes carefully chosen primary source documents. • thoughtfully uses an informal voice to make the informational piece interesting to young readers.	The writer correctly implements all conventions of grammar and sentence structure. The writer: • writes engaging and meaningful complete and compound sentences. • uses parts of speech in unique ways. • uses grammar conventions in clear and concise ways.	The writer correctly implements all conventions of mechanics (spelling, capitalization, punctuation). The writer: • always correctly indents paragraphs. • makes no, or few, mechanical mistakes, and any mistakes do not hinder overall meaning.
3	The writer's ideas are adequately organized and developed. The writer: • includes an introduction, or lead. • creates and maintains an organizational structure. • uses words and phrases that add effect and description to the informational piece. • includes a conclusion.	The writer demonstrates an adequate understanding of the features of an informational report. The writer: • develops the topic by including accurate information (facts, definitions, details). • includes graphics that support the information. • includes captions that explain each graphic feature. • includes one different viewpoint. • includes primary source documents. • uses an informal voice.	The writer implements most conventions of grammar and sentence structure. The writer: • writes adequate complete and compound sentences. • uses parts of speech correctly. • uses grammar conventions correctly.	The writer implements most conventions of mechanics (spelling, capitalization, punctuation). The writer: • correctly indents paragraphs most of the time. • makes occasional mechanical mistakes, but they do not hinder overall meaning.
2	The writer's ideas are somewhat organized and developed. The writer: • includes an introduction, or lead, that is weak. • attempts to create and maintain an organizational structure. Ideas are difficult to follow. • uses some words and phrases that add effect and description to the informational piece. • includes a weak conclusion.	The writer demonstrates some understanding of the features of an informational report. The writer: • somewhat develops the topic by including accurate information (facts, definitions, details). • includes few graphics to support the information. • includes some captions that explain the graphics. • attempts to include one different viewpoint. The viewpoint does not necessarily connect to the topic. • includes one primary source document. It may or may not connect to the topic. • attempts to use an informal voice.	The writer implements some conventions of grammar and sentence structure. The writer: • attempts to write complete and compound sentences. • uses some parts of speech correctly. • uses some grammar conventions correctly.	The writer implements some conventions of mechanics (spelling, capitalization, punctuation). The writer: • indents paragraphs some of the time. • makes many mechanical mistakes, and they hinder overall meaning.
1	The writer's ideas are disorganized and undeveloped. The writer: • does not include an introduction, or lead. • does not create nor maintain an organizational structure. Ideas are difficult to follow. • uses few, if any, words and phrases that add effect and description to the informational piece. • does not include a conclusion.	The writer demonstrates little, if any, understanding of the features of an informational report. The writer: • does not develop the topic. • includes few, if any, graphics to support the information. • includes few, if any, captions that explain the graphics. • does not include different viewpoints. • does not include primary source documents. • does not maintain an informal voice.	The writer implements few, if any, conventions of grammar and sentence structure. The writer: • does not write coherent complete and compound sentences. • rarely uses parts of speech correctly. • rarely uses grammar conventions correctly.	The writer implements few, if any, conventions of mechanics (spelling, capitalization, punctuation). The writer: • does not attempt to indent paragraphs. • makes many mechanical mistakes, and they hinder overall meaning.

Informative/Explanatory Report Checklist: Grade 2

Name _____ Date _____

Title _____

	Yes	No	Not Sure
1. My report has a strong lead.	—	—	—
2. I tell about my topic at the beginning of the report.	—	—	—
3. I use facts and details to support my ideas.	—	—	—
4. The information in my report is accurate.	—	—	—
5. My report is logically sequenced.	—	—	—
6. I include at least one graphic to support my information.	—	—	—
7. I include captions that explain each graphic.	—	—	—
8. My report includes at least one different viewpoint so that I do not sway my readers to think one way.	—	—	—
9. I use at least one primary source.	—	—	—
10. My report has a strong ending that keeps readers thinking.	—	—	—
11. I change the way I write my sentences.	—	—	—
12. I use adjectives and adverbs to make my informational text more interesting.	—	—	—

Quality Writing Checklist
I looked for and corrected . . .

	Yes	No	Not Sure
parts of speech (nouns, pronouns, verbs, adjectives, adverbs).	—	—	—
grammar.	—	—	—
indented paragraphs.	—	—	—
punctuation.	—	—	—
capitalization.	—	—	—
spelling.	—	—	—

Personal Narrative Rubric: Grade 2

Score	Planning and Implementation	Evidence of Genre Characteristics	Conventions of Grammar and Usage	Conventions of Mechanics
4	The writer's ideas are well organized and well developed. The writer: • recounts a well-elaborated event that is logically sequenced. • uses a variety of temporal words to show progression of events. • includes a variety of figurative language techniques such as onomatopoeia. • uses well-chosen descriptive words and phrases to describe people, places, and events. • begins the narrative with a strong lead that grabs readers' attention. • includes a strong ending that makes the reader think about the writer's ideas.	The writer demonstrates complete understanding of the features of a personal narrative. The writer: • focuses on one particular incident in the personal narrative. • includes specific details about the time, place, and people involved. • includes dialogue or expresses what people say. • uses well-chosen words to describe his or her own thoughts and feelings as well as the actual event. • uses conversational, everyday language well (voice).	The writer correctly implements all conventions of grammar and sentence structure. The writer: • writes engaging and meaningful complete and compound sentences. • uses parts of speech in unique ways. • uses grammar conventions in clear and concise ways.	The writer correctly implements all conventions of mechanics (spelling, capitalization, punctuation). The writer: • always correctly indents paragraphs. • makes no, or few, mechanical mistakes, and any mistakes do not hinder overall meaning.
3	The writer's ideas are adequately organized and developed. The writer: • recounts an adequately elaborated event that is logically sequenced. • uses many temporal words to show progression of events. • includes figurative language techniques such as onomatopoeia. • uses descriptive words and phrases to describe people, places, and events. • begins the narrative with a lead. • includes an ending.	The writer demonstrates adequate understanding of the features of a personal narrative. The writer: • focuses on one particular incident in the personal narrative. • includes details about the time, place, and people involved. • includes dialogue or expresses what people say. • describes his/her own thoughts and feelings as well as the actual event. • uses conversational, everyday language adequately (voice).	The writer implements most conventions of grammar and sentence structure. The writer: • writes adequate complete and compound sentences. • uses parts of speech correctly. • uses grammar conventions correctly.	The writer implements most conventions of mechanics (spelling, capitalization, punctuation). The writer: • correctly indents paragraphs most of the time. • makes occasional mechanical mistakes, but they do not hinder overall meaning.
2	The writer's ideas are somewhat organized and developed. The writer: • attempts to recount an event that may or may not be logically sequenced. • uses few temporal words. Progression of events is confusing. • inadequately uses figurative language. • uses some descriptive words and phrases to describe people, places, and events. • begins the narrative with a weak lead. • includes a weak ending that may or may not connect with the event.	The writer demonstrates some understanding of the features of a personal narrative. The writer: • attempts to focus on one particular incident in the personal narrative. • includes some details about the time, place, and people involved. • inadequately attempts dialogue or expresses what people say. • inadequately attempts to describe his/her own thoughts and feelings as well as the actual event. • inadequately attempts to use conversational, everyday language (voice).	The writer implements some conventions of grammar and sentence structure. The writer: • attempts to write complete and compound sentences. • uses some parts of speech correctly. • uses some grammar conventions correctly.	The writer implements some conventions of mechanics (spelling, capitalization, punctuation). The writer: • indents paragraphs some of the time. • makes many mechanical mistakes, and they hinder overall meaning.
1	The writer's ideas are disorganized and undeveloped. The writer: • attempts to recount an event. It is not logically sequenced. • uses few, if any, temporal words. Progression of events is confusing. • does not use figurative language. • uses few, if any, descriptive words and phrases to describe people, places, and events. • does not include a lead that connects to the event, or does not include a lead at all. • does not include an ending that connects with the event, or does not include an ending at all.	The writer demonstrates little, if any, understanding of the features of a personal narrative. The writer: • does not attempt to focus on one particular event in the personal narrative. • includes few, if any, details about the time, place, and people involved. • does not attempt to include dialogue or express what people say. • does not attempt to describe his/her own thoughts and feelings or to describe the actual event. • does not establish an obvious voice.	The writer implements few, if any, conventions of grammar and sentence structure. The writer: • does not write coherent complete and compound sentences. • rarely uses parts of speech correctly. • rarely uses grammar conventions correctly.	The writer implements few, if any, conventions of mechanics (spelling, capitalization, punctuation). The writer: • does not attempt to indent paragraphs. • makes many mechanical mistakes, and they hinder overall meaning.

Personal Narrative Checklist: Grade 2

Name _____ Date _____

Title _____

	Yes	No	Not Sure
1. My narrative has a strong lead.	___	___	___
2. My narrative focuses on one event in my life.	___	___	___
3. I include specific details about the time, place, and people involved.	___	___	___
4. I include dialogue or expressed what people said.	___	___	___
5. My narrative is logically sequenced.	___	___	___
6. My narrative uses sequence words.	___	___	___
7. I include my own thoughts and feelings.	___	___	___
8. My narrative has a strong ending.	___	___	___
9. I tell my story using my everyday voice.	___	___	___
10. I use describing words, including adjectives and adverbs, that "show, not tell" my story.	___	___	___
11. I use figurative language, including onomatopoeia, to make my narrative interesting.	___	___	___
12. I use simple and compound sentences.	___	___	___

Quality Writing Checklist
I looked for and corrected . . .

	Yes	No	Not Sure
parts of speech (nouns, pronouns, verbs, adjectives, adverbs).	___	___	___
grammar.	___	___	___
indented paragraphs.	___	___	___
punctuation.	___	___	___
capitalization.	___	___	___
spelling.	___	___	___

Opinion Rubric: Grade 3

Score	Planning and Implementation	Evidence of Genre Characteristics	Conventions of Grammar and Usage	Conventions of Mechanics
4	The writer's ideas are well organized and well developed. The writer: • maintains a meaningful organizational structure. • clearly maintains the opinion throughout the text. • uses well-chosen words and phrases that add effect to the opinion piece.	The writer demonstrates complete understanding of the features of an opinion text. The writer: • clearly introduces the topic. • states an opinion about the topic. • includes at least one reason for the opinion based on inferences made about the topic. • includes purposefully chosen text evidence that supports the reason(s). • uses a wide variety of linking words and phrases that connect reasons with evidence. • includes an effective concluding sentence or paragraph that makes the reader think about the writer's ideas. • consistently uses third person and present tense.	The writer correctly implements all conventions of grammar and sentence structure. The writer: • uses a variety of sentence structures including simple, compound, and complex sentences. • uses parts of speech in unique ways. • uses grammar conventions in clear and concise ways.	The writer correctly implements all conventions of mechanics (spelling, capitalization, punctuation). The writer: • always correctly indents paragraphs. • makes no, or few, mechanical mistakes, and any mistakes do not hinder overall meaning.
3	The writer's ideas are adequately organized and developed. The writer: • creates and maintains an organizational structure. • maintains the opinion throughout the text. • uses words and phrases that add effect to the opinion piece.	The writer demonstrates an adequate understanding of the features of an opinion text. The writer: • clearly introduces the topic. • states an opinion about the topic. • includes at least one reason for the opinion. • includes text evidence that supports the reason(s). • uses linking words and phrases that connect reasons with evidence. • includes a concluding sentence or paragraph. • uses third person and present tense most of the time.	The writer implements most conventions of grammar and sentence structure. The writer: • uses varied sentence structures including simple, compound, and complex sentences. • uses correct parts of speech most of the time. • uses correct grammar conventions most of the time.	The writer implements most conventions of mechanics (spelling, capitalization, punctuation). The writer: • correctly indents paragraphs most of the time. • makes occasional mechanical mistakes, but they do not hinder overall meaning.
2	The writer's ideas are somewhat organized and developed. The writer: • attempts to create an organizational structure. Ideas are difficult to follow. • inadequately maintains the opinion throughout the text. Text suggests the writer does not understand the stated opinion. • uses few words and phrases that add effect to the opinion piece.	The writer demonstrates some understanding of the features of an opinion text. The writer: • attempts to introduce the topic. • states a weak opinion about the topic. • includes a reason for the opinion. • includes some text evidence that supports the reason, but evidence is weak. • uses some linking words and phrases that connect reasons with evidence. • includes a weak concluding sentence or paragraph. • uses third person and present tense some of the time.	The writer implements some conventions of grammar and sentence structure. The writer: • attempts to use sentence structures including simple, compound, and complex sentences. • uses correct parts of speech some of the time. • uses correct grammar conventions some of the time.	The writer implements some conventions of mechanics (spelling, capitalization, punctuation). The writer: • indents paragraphs some of the time. • makes many mechanical mistakes, and they sometimes hinder overall meaning.
1	The writer's ideas are disorganized and undeveloped. The writer: • does not attempt to create an organizational structure. • does not maintain the opinion throughout the text. • uses few, if any, words and phrases that add effect to the opinion piece.	The writer demonstrates little, if any, understanding of the features of an opinion text. The writer: • does not introduce the topic. • states an unclear opinion. • includes a reason for the opinion. The reason may or may not be connected to the topic. • includes little, if any, text evidence that supports the reason. • uses few, if any, linking words and phrases that connect reasons with evidence. • does not include a concluding sentence or paragraph. • rarely uses third person and present tense correctly.	The writer implements few, if any, conventions of grammar and sentence structure. The writer: • does not vary sentence structures (simple, compound, and complex sentences). • rarely uses correct parts of speech. • rarely uses correct grammar conventions.	The writer implements few, if any, conventions of mechanics (spelling, capitalization, punctuation). The writer: • does not attempt to indent paragraphs. • makes many mechanical mistakes, and they hinder overall meaning.

Opinion Checklist: Grade 3

Name _____   Date _____

Title _____

		Yes	No	Not Sure
1.	I introduce my topic.	___	___	___
2.	I state my opinion at the beginning of my paper.	___	___	___
3.	I include reasons for my opinion based on my own thoughts about the topic.	___	___	___
4.	I use evidence from the text to support my opinion.	___	___	___
5.	I use linking words and phrases to connect reasons and evidence.	___	___	___
6.	I include a concluding sentence or paragraph that makes my readers think.	___	___	___
7.	My opinion follows an organized structure.	___	___	___
8.	I choose words that make sense and make my opinion interesting.	___	___	___
9.	I do not change my opinion.	___	___	___
10.	I use different types of sentences.	___	___	___
11.	I use third person and present tense.	___	___	___

Quality Writing Checklist
I looked for and corrected . . .

	Yes	No	Not Sure
parts of speech (nouns, pronouns, verbs, adjectives, adverbs).	___	___	___
grammar.	___	___	___
indented paragraphs.	___	___	___
punctuation.	___	___	___
capitalization.	___	___	___
spelling.	___	___	___

Informative/Explanatory Report Rubric: Grade 3

Score	Planning and Implementation	Evidence of Genre Characteristics	Conventions of Grammar and Usage	Conventions of Mechanics
4	The writer's ideas are well organized and well developed. The writer: • grabs readers' attention with a strong lead. • creates and maintains a meaningful organizational structure by introducing the topic and grouping related information. • consistently varies sentence structure (adding detail, combining sentences, starting sentences with different words) to facilitate clear ideas. • uses a wide variety of linking words and phrases to connect ideas. • uses well-chosen words and phrases that add effect and description to the informational piece. • includes a strong conclusion that keeps readers thinking.	The writer demonstrates complete understanding of the features of an informational report. The writer: • thoroughly develops the topic by including accurate information (facts, definitions, details). • includes unique graphics that support the information. • includes thoughtfully worded captions that explain each graphic feature. • includes one or more different viewpoints so readers can draw their own conclusions. • includes carefully chosen primary source documents. • consistently maintains a formal voice.	The writer correctly implements all conventions. The writer: • uses a variety of sentence structures including simple, compound, and complex sentences. • uses parts of speech in unique ways. • uses grammar conventions in clear and concise ways.	The writer correctly implements all conventions. The writer: • always correctly indents paragraphs. • makes no, or few, mechanical mistakes, and any mistakes do not hinder overall meaning.
3	The writer's ideas are adequately organized and developed. The writer: • includes an introduction, or lead. • creates and maintains an organizational structure. • varies sentence structure (adding detail, combining sentences, starting sentences with different words) to facilitate clear ideas. • uses linking words and phrases to connect ideas. • uses words and phrases that add effect and description to the informational piece. • includes a conclusion.	The writer demonstrates an adequate understanding of the features of an informational report. The writer: • develops the topic by including accurate information (facts, definitions, details). • includes graphics that support the information. • includes captions that explain each graphic feature. • includes one different viewpoint. • includes primary sources. • maintains a formal voice.	The writer implements most conventions. The writer: • uses varied sentence structures including simple, compound, and complex sentences. • uses correct parts of speech most of the time. • uses correct grammar conventions most of the time.	The writer implements most conventions. The writer: • correctly indents paragraphs most of the time. • makes occasional mechanical mistakes, but they do not hinder overall meaning.
2	The writer's ideas are somewhat organized and developed. The writer: • includes an introduction, or lead, that is weak. • attempts to create and maintain an organizational structure. Ideas are difficult to follow. • attempts to vary sentence structure (adding detail, combining sentences, starting sentences with different words). Attempts may or may not aid meaning. • uses some linking words and phrases to connect ideas. • uses some words and phrases that add effect and description to the piece. • includes a weak conclusion.	The writer demonstrates some understanding of the features of an informational report. The writer: • somewhat develops the topic by including accurate information. • includes few graphics to support the information. • includes some captions that explain the graphics. • attempts to include one different viewpoint. The viewpoint does not necessarily connect to the topic. • includes one primary source. It may or may not connect to the topic. • inconsistently maintains a formal voice.	The writer implements some conventions. The writer: • attempts to use varied sentence structures including simple, compound, and complex sentences. • uses correct parts of speech some of the time. • uses correct grammar conventions some of the time.	The writer implements some conventions. The writer: • indents paragraphs some of the time. • makes many mechanical mistakes, and they hinder overall meaning.
1	The writer's ideas are disorganized and undeveloped. The writer: • does not include an introduction. • does not create nor maintain an organizational structure. Ideas are difficult to follow. • does not vary sentence structure (adding detail, combining sentences, starting sentences with different words). • uses few, if any, linking words and phrases to connect ideas. • uses few, if any, words and phrases that add effect and description to the piece. • does not include a conclusion.	The writer demonstrates little, if any, understanding of the features of an informational report. The writer: • does not develop the topic. • includes few, if any, graphics to support the information. • includes few, if any, captions that explain the graphics. • does not include different viewpoints. • does not include primary source documents. • does not maintain a formal voice.	The writer implements few, if any, conventions. The writer: • does not vary sentence structures (simple, compound, and complex sentences). • rarely uses correct parts of speech. • rarely uses correct grammar conventions.	The writer implements few, if any, conventions. The writer: • does not attempt to indent paragraphs. • makes many mechanical mistakes, and they hinder overall meaning.

Informative/Explanatory Report Checklist: Grade 3

Name _____ Date _____

Title _____

	Yes	No	Not Sure
1. I introduce my topic and use words that grab my readers' attention.	—	—	—
2. I keep my paper organized by grouping information together in a way that makes sense.	—	—	—
3. The information in my report is accurate.	—	—	—
4. I use facts and details to support my points.	—	—	—
5. I include graphics to support my information.	—	—	—
6. I include captions that explain each graphic.	—	—	—
7. I use linking words and phrases to connect ideas.	—	—	—
8. My report includes different viewpoints so that I do not sway my readers to think one way.	—	—	—
9. I include a strong conclusion that keeps my readers thinking.	—	—	—
10. I choose words that make my text interesting to read and easy to understand.	—	—	—
11. I use at least one primary source.	—	—	—
12. I use different types of sentences.	—	—	—
13. I left "I" behind in my report and use a formal voice.	—	—	—

Quality Writing Checklist
I looked for and corrected . . .

	Yes	No	Not Sure
parts of speech (nouns, pronouns, verbs, adjectives, adverbs).	—	—	—
grammar.	—	—	—
indented paragraphs.	—	—	—
punctuation.	—	—	—
capitalization.	—	—	—
spelling.	—	—	—

Personal Narrative Rubric: Grade 3

Score	Planning and Implementation	Evidence of Genre Characteristics	Conventions of Grammar and Usage	Conventions of Mechanics
4	The writer's ideas are well organized and well developed. The writer: • recounts a well-elaborated event that is logically sequenced. • uses a variety of temporal words to show progression of events. • uses well-chosen descriptive words and phrases to describe people, places, and events. • begins the narrative with a strong lead that grabs readers' attention. • includes a strong ending that makes the reader think about the writer's incident.	The writer demonstrates complete understanding of the features of a personal narrative. The writer: • focuses on one particular incident in the personal narrative. • includes specific details about the time, place, and people involved. • effectively includes dialogue or expresses what people say in a way that brings the story to life. • uses well-chosen words to describe his/her own thoughts and feelings as well as the actual event. • makes a strong connection with the reader by using an informal, personal voice.	The writer correctly implements all conventions of grammar and sentence structure. The writer: • uses a variety of sentence structures including simple, compound, and complex sentences. • uses parts of speech in unique ways. • uses grammar conventions in clear and concise ways.	The writer correctly implements all conventions of mechanics (spelling, capitalization, punctuation). The writer: • always correctly indents paragraphs. • makes no, or few, mechanical mistakes, and any mistakes do not hinder overall meaning.
3	The writer's ideas are adequately organized and developed. The writer: • recounts an adequately elaborated event that is logically sequenced. • uses many temporal words to show progression of events. • uses descriptive words and phrases to describe people, places, and events. • begins the narrative with a lead. • includes an ending.	The writer demonstrates adequate understanding of the features of a personal narrative. The writer: • focuses on one particular incident in the personal narrative. • includes details about the time, place, and people involved. • includes dialogue or expresses what people say. • describes his/her own thoughts and feelings as well as the actual event. • makes a connection with the reader by using a personal voice.	The writer implements most conventions of grammar and sentence structure. The writer: • uses varied sentence structures including simple, compound, and complex sentences. • uses correct parts of speech most of the time. • uses correct grammar conventions most of the time.	The writer implements most conventions of mechanics (spelling, capitalization, punctuation). The writer: • correctly indents paragraphs most of the time. • makes occasional mechanical mistakes, but they do not hinder overall meaning.
2	The writer's ideas are somewhat organized and developed. The writer: • attempts to recount an event that may or may not be logically sequenced. • uses some temporal words to show progression of events. Progression of events is confusing. • inadequately describes people, places, and events. • begins the narrative with a weak lead. • includes a weak ending.	The writer demonstrates some understanding of the features of a personal narrative. The writer: • attempts to focus on one particular incident in the personal narrative. • includes few details about the time, place, and people involved. • includes some dialogue or attempts to express what people say. • inadequately describes his/her own thoughts and feelings as well as the actual event. • inadequately connects with the reader because of a weak personal voice.	The writer implements some conventions of grammar and sentence structure. The writer: • attempts to use sentence structures including simple, compound, and complex sentences. • uses correct parts of speech some of the time. • uses correct grammar conventions some of the time.	The writer implements some conventions of mechanics (spelling, capitalization, punctuation). The writer: • indents paragraphs some of the time. • makes many mechanical mistakes, and they hinder overall meaning.
1	The writer's ideas are disorganized and undeveloped. The writer: • attempts to recount an event. It is not logically sequenced. • uses few, if any, temporal words to show progression of events. Progression of events is confusing. • does not describe people, places, and events. • does not include a lead. • does not include an ending.	The writer demonstrates little, if any, understanding of the features of a personal narrative. The writer: • does not focus on one particular incident in the personal narrative. • includes few, if any, details about the time, place, and people involved. • includes little, if any, dialogue or does not express what people say. • does not describe his/her own thoughts and feelings as well as the actual event. • does not connect to the reader with voice.	The writer implements few, if any, conventions of grammar and sentence structure. The writer: • does not vary sentence structures (simple, compound, and complex sentences). • rarely uses correct parts of speech. • rarely uses correct grammar conventions.	The writer implements few, if any, conventions of mechanics (spelling, capitalization, punctuation). The writer: • does not attempt to indent paragraphs. • makes many mechanical mistakes, and they hinder overall meaning.

Personal Narrative Checklist: Grade 3

Name _____ Date _____

Title _____

	Yes	No	Not Sure
1. My narrative has a strong lead that catches the reader's attention.	___	___	___
2. My narrative focuses on one event in my life.	___	___	___
3. I include specific details about the time, place, and people involved.	___	___	___
4. I include dialogue or express what people said.	___	___	___
5. My narrative is logically sequenced.	___	___	___
6. My narrative uses sequence words.	___	___	___
7. I include my own thoughts and feelings.	___	___	___
8. My narrative has a strong ending.	___	___	___
9. I tell my story using my everyday voice.	___	___	___
10. I use describing words, including adjectives and adverbs, to tell my story.	___	___	___
11. I use simple, compound, and complex sentences.	___	___	___

Quality Writing Checklist
I looked for and corrected . . .

	Yes	No	Not Sure
parts of speech (nouns, pronouns, verbs, adjectives, adverbs).	___	___	___
grammar.	___	___	___
indented paragraphs.	___	___	___
punctuation.	___	___	___
capitalization.	___	___	___
spelling.	___	___	___

Opinion Rubric: Grade 4

Score	Planning and Implementation	Evidence of Genre Characteristics	Conventions of Grammar and Usage	Conventions of Mechanics
4	The writer's ideas are well organized and well developed. The writer: • creates and maintains a meaningful organizational structure. • effectively groups related ideas. • uses well-chosen words and phrases that add effect to the opinion piece. • clearly maintains the opinion throughout the text.	The writer demonstrates complete understanding of the features of an opinion text. The writer: • clearly introduces the topic with a strong lead that gets readers' attention. • states an opinion that shows a complete understanding of the topic. • includes multiple reasons for the opinion based on inferences made about the topic. • includes purposefully chosen text evidence to support reasons. • uses a wide variety of linking words and phrases that connect reasons with evidence. • includes an effective concluding sentence or paragraph that makes the reader think about the writer's ideas. • has a voice that shows a strong conviction about the opinion.	The writer correctly implements all conventions. The writer: • produces well-developed complete sentences. • efficiently revises and corrects sentence fragments and run-ons. • uses parts of speech in unique ways. • uses grammar conventions in clear and concise ways.	The writer correctly implements all conventions. The writer: • always correctly indents paragraphs. • makes no, or few, mechanical mistakes, and they do not hinder overall meaning.
3	The writer's ideas are adequately organized and developed. The writer: • creates and maintains an organizational structure. • groups connected ideas most of the time. • uses words and phrases that add effect to the opinion piece. • maintains the opinion throughout the text.	The writer demonstrates an adequate understanding of the features of an opinion text. The writer: • introduces the topic with a lead. • states an opinion about the topic. • includes at least two reasons for the opinion. • includes text evidence that supports each reason. • uses linking words and phrases that connect reasons with evidence. • includes a concluding sentence or paragraph. • has a voice that shows conviction about the opinion.	The writer implements most conventions. The writer: • produces complete sentences. • revises and corrects sentence fragments and run-ons most of the time. • uses correct parts of speech most of the time. • uses correct grammar conventions most of the time.	The writer implements most conventions. The writer: • correctly indents paragraphs most of the time. • makes occasional mechanical mistakes, but they do not hinder overall meaning.
2	The writer's ideas are somewhat organized and developed. The writer: • attempts to create an organizational structure. Ideas are difficult to follow. • attempts to group connected ideas. • uses few words and phrases that add effect to the opinion piece. • inadequately maintains the opinion throughout the text. Text suggests the writer does not understand the stated opinion.	The writer demonstrates some understanding of the features of an opinion text. The writer: • attempts to introduce the topic. Lead is weak. • states a weak opinion about the topic. • includes one reason for the opinion. • includes some text evidence that supports the reason, but evidence is weak. • uses some linking words and phrases that connect reasons with evidence. • includes a weak concluding sentence or paragraph. • has a voice that shows some conviction about the opinion.	The writer implements some conventions. The writer: • produces complete sentences some of the time. • revises and corrects sentence fragments and run-ons some of the time. • uses correct parts of speech some of the time. • uses correct grammar conventions some of the time.	The writer implements some conventions. The writer: • indents paragraphs some of the time. • makes some mechanical mistakes, and they hinder overall meaning.
1	The writer's ideas are disorganized and undeveloped. The writer: • does not attempt to create an organizational structure. • does not group connected ideas. • uses few, if any, words and phrases that add effect to the opinion piece. • does not maintain the opinion throughout the text.	The writer demonstrates little, if any, understanding of the features of an opinion. The writer: • does not introduce the topic. There is no obvious lead. • states an unclear opinion. • includes one reason, if any, for the opinion. • includes little, if any, text evidence that supports the reason. • uses few, if any, linking words and phrases that connect reasons with evidence. • does not include a concluding sentence or paragraph. • has a voice that shows little, if any, conviction about the opinion.	The writer implements few, if any, conventions. The writer: • rarely produces complete sentences. • rarely revises and corrects sentence fragments and run-ons. • rarely uses correct parts of speech. • rarely uses correct grammar conventions.	The writer implements few, if any, conventions. The writer: • does not attempt to indent paragraphs. • makes many mechanical mistakes, and they hinder overall meaning.

Opinion Checklist: Grade 4

Name _____ Date _____

Title _____

		Yes	No	Not Sure
1.	I introduce my topic with a lead that gets my readers' attention.	___	___	___
2.	I state my opinion at the beginning of my paper.	___	___	___
3.	I include reasons for my opinion based on my own thoughts about the topic.	___	___	___
4.	I group connected ideas together.	___	___	___
5.	I use evidence from the text to support my opinion.	___	___	___
6.	I use linking words and phrases to connect reasons and evidence.	___	___	___
7.	I include a concluding sentence or paragraph that makes my readers think.	___	___	___
8.	My opinion follows an organized structure.	___	___	___
9.	I choose words that make sense and make my opinion interesting.	___	___	___
10.	I do not change my opinion.	___	___	___
11.	I use different types of sentences.	___	___	___
12.	I use my voice to show people how much I care about my opinion.	___	___	___

Quality Writing Checklist
I looked for and corrected . . .

	Yes	No	Not Sure
sentence fragments and run-ons.	___	___	___
parts of speech (pronouns, auxiliaries, adjectives, prepositions).	___	___	___
grammar.	___	___	___
indented paragraphs.	___	___	___
punctuation.	___	___	___
capitalization.	___	___	___
spelling.	___	___	___

Informative/Explanatory Report Rubric: Grade 4

Score	Planning and Implementation	Evidence of Genre Characteristics	Conventions of Grammar and Usage	Conventions of Mechanics
4	The writer's ideas are well organized and well developed. The writer: • thoroughly researches the topic before writing. • includes an introduction, or lead, that grabs readers' attention. • creates and maintains a meaningful organizational structure by introducing the topic and grouping related information. • consistently varies sentence structure to facilitate clear ideas. • uses a wide variety of linking words and phrases to link ideas within categories of information. • uses well-chosen words and phrases and domain-specific vocabulary that add effect and description to the piece. • includes a strong conclusion that keeps readers thinking.	The writer demonstrates complete understanding of the features of an informational report. The writer: • thoroughly develops the topic by including facts, definitions, details, and examples. • includes unique text and graphic features (headings, charts, illustrations, etc.) that support the information. • includes thoughtfully worded captions that explain each graphic feature. • includes one or more different viewpoints so readers can draw their own conclusions. • includes carefully chosen primary sources. • consistently maintains a formal voice.	The writer correctly implements all conventions. The writer: • produces well-developed complete sentences. • efficiently revises and corrects sentence fragments and run-ons. • uses parts of speech in unique ways. • uses grammar conventions in clear and concise ways.	The writer correctly implements all conventions. The writer: • always correctly indents paragraphs. • makes no, or few, mechanical mistakes, and they do not hinder overall meaning.
3	The writer's ideas are adequately organized and developed. The writer: • researches the topic before writing. • includes an introduction, or lead. • creates and maintains an organizational structure and groups related information into paragraphs or sections. • varies sentence structure to facilitate clear ideas. • uses linking words and phrases to link ideas within categories of information. • uses words and phrases and domain-specific words that add effect and description to the informational piece. • includes a conclusion.	The writer demonstrates an adequate understanding of the features of an informational report. The writer: • develops the topic by including facts, definitions, details, and examples. • includes text and graphic features (headings, charts, illustrations, etc.) that support the information. • includes captions that explain the graphics. • includes one different viewpoint. • includes primary source documents. • maintains a formal voice.	The writer implements most conventions. The writer: • produces complete sentences. • revises and corrects sentence fragments and run-ons most of the time. • uses correct parts of speech most of the time. • uses correct grammar conventions most of the time.	The writer implements most conventions. The writer: • correctly indents paragraphs most of the time. • makes occasional mechanical mistakes, but they do not hinder overall meaning.
2	The writer's ideas are somewhat organized and developed. The writer: • does some research on the project. • includes an introduction, or lead, that is weak. • attempts to create and maintain an organizational structure. Though the writer attempts to group related ideas, they are difficult to follow. • attempts to vary sentence structure. Attempt does not aid understanding. • uses some linking words and phrases to link ideas within categories of information. • uses some words and phrases that add effect and description. Domain-specific words may or may not be included. • includes a weak conclusion.	The writer demonstrates some understanding of the features of an informational report. The writer: • somewhat develops the topic by including facts, definitions, details, etc. • includes few text and graphic features to support the information. • includes some captions that explain the graphics. Captions may or may not adequately address the graphic. • attempts to include one different viewpoint. The viewpoint does not necessarily connect to the topic. • includes one primary source document. It may or may not connect to the topic. • inconsistently maintains a formal voice.	The writer implements some conventions. The writer: • produces complete sentences some of the time. • revises and corrects sentence fragments and run-ons some of the time. • uses correct parts of speech some of the time. • uses correct grammar conventions some of the time.	The writer implements some conventions. The writer: • indents paragraphs some of the time. • makes many mechanical mistakes, and they sometimes hinder overall meaning.
1	The writer's ideas are disorganized and undeveloped. The writer: • does very little research on the topic. • does not include an introduction, or lead. • does not create or maintain an organizational structure. Ideas may be grouped, but they are difficult to follow. • does not vary sentence structure. • uses few, if any, linking words and phrases to link ideas. • uses few, if any, words and phrases that add effect and description. Writer includes few domain-specific words. • does not include a conclusion.	The writer demonstrates little, if any, understanding of the features of an informational report. The writer: • does not develop the topic. • includes few, if any, text and graphic features to support the information. • includes few, if any, captions. Captions do not necessarily explain the graphics. • does not include different viewpoints. • does not include primary sources. • does not maintain a formal voice.	The writer implements few, if any, conventions. The writer: • rarely produces complete sentences. • rarely revises and corrects fragments and run-ons. • rarely uses correct parts of speech. • rarely uses correct grammar conventions.	The writer implements few, if any, conventions. The writer: • does not attempt to indent paragraphs. • makes many mechanical mistakes that hinder overall meaning.

Informative/Explanatory Report Checklist: Grade 4

Name _____ Date _____

Title _____

	Yes	No	Not Sure
1. I researched my topic and organized my information into notes that helped me write my paper.	—	—	—
2. I introduce my topic and use words that grab my readers' attention.	—	—	—
3. I keep my paper organized by grouping information together in a way that makes sense. I use paragraphs and sections.	—	—	—
4. I use headings to organize my sections.	—	—	—
5. The information in my report is accurate.	—	—	—
6. I support my points with facts, definitions, and details.	—	—	—
7. I include graphics to support my information.	—	—	—
8. I include captions that explain each graphic.	—	—	—
9. I use linking words and phrases to connect ideas.	—	—	—
10. My report includes different viewpoints so that I do not sway my readers to think one way.	—	—	—
11. I include a strong conclusion that keeps my readers thinking.	—	—	—
12. I choose words that make my text interesting to read and easy to understand. I include words that connect to the topic.	—	—	—
13. I use at least one primary source.	—	—	—
14. I use a formal voice.	—	—	—

Quality Writing Checklist
I looked for and corrected . . .

	Yes	No	Not Sure
sentence fragments and run-ons.	—	—	—
parts of speech (pronouns, auxiliaries, adjectives, prepositions).	—	—	—
grammar.	—	—	—
indented paragraphs.	—	—	—
punctuation.	—	—	—
capitalization.	—	—	—
spelling.	—	—	—

Personal Narrative Rubric: Grade 4

Score	Planning and Implementation	Evidence of Genre Characteristics	Conventions of Grammar and Usage	Conventions of Mechanics
4	The writer's ideas are well organized and well developed. The writer: • effectively orients the reader by establishing a well-elaborated situation. • recounts a well-elaborated event that is logically sequenced. • uses a variety of transition words and phrases to manage the sequence of events. • uses well-chosen concrete words and phrases and sensory details. • includes figurative language, including idioms, to make the narrative more interesting. • grabs readers' attention with a strong lead. • includes a strong ending that naturally makes the reader reflect on the narrative.	The writer demonstrates complete understanding of the features of a personal narrative. The writer: • focuses on one particular incident in the personal narrative. • includes specific details about the time, place, and people involved. • effectively includes dialogue or expresses what people say in a way that brings the story to life. • uses well-chosen words to describe his/her own convictions, thoughts, and feelings as well as the actual event. • makes a connection with the reader by using kid-friendly language (voice).	The writer correctly implements all conventions. The writer: • produces well-developed complete sentences. • efficiently revises and corrects sentence fragments and run-ons. • effectively and purposefully breaks sentence structure rules to enhance meaning. • uses parts of speech in unique ways. • uses grammar conventions in clear and concise ways.	The writer correctly implements all conventions. The writer: • always correctly indents paragraphs. • makes no, or few, mechanical mistakes, and they do not hinder overall meaning.
3	The writer's ideas are adequately organized and developed. The writer: • establishes a situation. • recounts an adequately elaborated event that is logically sequenced. • uses transition words and phrases to manage the sequence of events. • uses descriptive words and phrases and sensory details. • includes figurative language including idioms. • begins the narrative with a lead. • includes an ending.	The writer demonstrates adequate understanding of the features of a personal narrative. The writer: • focuses on one particular incident in the personal narrative. • includes details about the time, place, and people involved. • includes dialogue or expresses what people say. • describes his/her convictions, thoughts, and feelings as well as the event. • uses kid-friendly language (voice).	The writer implements most conventions. The writer: • produces complete sentences. • revises and corrects sentence fragments and run-ons most of the time. • purposefully breaks sentence structure rules to enhance meaning. • uses correct parts of speech most of the time. • uses correct grammar conventions most of the time.	The writer implements most conventions. The writer: • correctly indents paragraphs most of the time. • makes occasional mechanical mistakes, but they do not hinder overall meaning.
2	The writer's ideas are somewhat organized and developed. The writer: • attempts to establish a situation. • attempts to recount an event. Some parts are logically sequenced. • uses some transition words and phrases to manage the sequence of events. Progression of events is confusing. • inadequately describes people, places, and events. • may or may not include idioms. • begins the narrative with a weak lead. • includes a weak ending.	The writer demonstrates some understanding of the features of a personal narrative. The writer: • attempts to focus on one particular incident in the personal narrative. • includes few details about the time, place, and people involved. • includes some dialogue or attempts to express what people say. • inadequately describes his/her own convictions, thoughts, and feelings as well as the actual event. • attempts to use kid-friendly language (voice).	The writer implements some conventions. The writer: • produces complete sentences some of the time. • revises and corrects sentence fragments and run-ons some of the time. • attempts to break sentence structure rules. Meaning may or may not be enhanced. • uses correct parts of speech some of the time. • uses correct grammar conventions some of the time.	The writer implements some conventions. The writer: • indents paragraphs some of the time. • makes many mechanical mistakes, and they sometimes hinder overall meaning.
1	The writer's ideas are disorganized and undeveloped. The writer: • does not establish a situation, leaving the reader confused as to the topic. • attempts to recount an event. Event is not logically sequenced. • rarely uses transition words and phrases to manage the sequence of events. Progression of events is confusing. • does not describe people, places, and events. • does not include idioms. • does not have a lead. • does not have an ending.	The writer demonstrates little, if any, understanding of the features of a personal narrative. The writer: • does not focus on one particular incident in the personal narrative. • includes few, if any, details about the time, place, and people involved. • includes little, if any, dialogue or does not express what people say. • does not describe his/her own convictions, thoughts, and feelings as well as the actual event. • does not purposefully use kid-friendly language (voice).	The writer implements few, if any, conventions. The writer: • rarely produces complete sentences. • rarely revises and corrects sentence fragments and run-ons. • attempts to break sentence structure rules. Meaning is hindered. • rarely uses correct parts of speech. • rarely uses correct grammar conventions.	The writer implements few, if any, conventions. The writer: • does not attempt to indent paragraphs. • makes many mechanical mistakes, and they hinder overall meaning.

Personal Narrative Checklist: Grade 4

Name _____ Date _____

Title _____

		Yes	No	Not Sure
1.	My narrative has a strong lead that catches the reader's attention.	—	—	—
2.	My narrative focuses on one event in my life.	—	—	—
3.	I include specific details about the time, place, and people involved.	—	—	—
4.	I include dialogue or express what people said.	—	—	—
5.	My narrative is logically sequenced.	—	—	—
6.	My narrative uses sequence words.	—	—	—
7.	I include my own convictions, thoughts, and feelings.	—	—	—
8.	My narrative has a strong ending.	—	—	—
9.	I tell my personal narrative using kid-friendly language.	—	—	—
10.	I use describing words, including adjectives and adverbs, to tell my story.	—	—	—
11.	I use figurative language, including idioms, to make my personal narrative more interesting.	—	—	—
12.	I broke sentence rules when necessary to make my personal narrative more interesting.	—	—	—

Quality Writing Checklist
I looked for and corrected . . .

	Yes	No	Not Sure
sentence fragments and run-ons.	—	—	—
parts of speech (pronouns, auxiliaries, adjectives, prepositions).	—	—	—
grammar.	—	—	—
indented paragraphs.	—	—	—
punctuation.	—	—	—
capitalization.	—	—	—
spelling.	—	—	—

Opinion Rubric: Grade 5

Score	Planning and Implementation	Evidence of Genre Characteristics	Conventions of Grammar and Usage	Conventions of Mechanics
4	The writer's ideas are well organized and well developed. The writer: • creates and maintains a meaningful organizational structure. • effectively groups related ideas to support the opinion. • uses well-chosen words and phrases that add effect to the opinion piece. • clearly maintains the opinion throughout the text.	The writer demonstrates complete understanding of the features of an opinion text. The writer: • clearly introduces the topic with a strong lead. • states an opinion that shows a full understanding of the topic. • includes multiple, logically ordered reasons for the opinion based on inferences made about the topic. • includes well-chosen text evidence that supports each reason. • uses a wide variety of linking words and phrases that connect reasons with evidence. • includes an effective concluding sentence or paragraph that makes the reader think about the writer's ideas. • has a voice that shows a strong conviction about the opinion.	The writer correctly implements all conventions. The writer: • uses parts of speech in unique ways. • uses grammar conventions in clear and concise ways. • expands, combines, and reduces sentences in unique ways that enhance meaning and style.	The writer correctly implements all conventions. The writer: • always correctly indents paragraphs. • makes no, or few, mechanical mistakes, and they do not hinder overall meaning.
3	The writer's ideas are adequately organized and developed. The writer: • creates and maintains an organizational structure. • groups related ideas to support the opinion most of the time. • uses words and phrases that add effect to the opinion piece. • maintains the opinion throughout the text.	The writer demonstrates an adequate understanding of the features of an opinion text. The writer: • introduces the topic with a lead. • states an opinion about the topic. • includes at least two logically ordered reasons for the opinion. • includes text evidence that supports each reason. • uses linking words and phrases that connect reasons with evidence. • includes a concluding sentence or paragraph. • has a voice that shows conviction about the opinion.	The writer implements most conventions. The writer: • uses parts of speech correctly. • uses grammar conventions correctly. • adequately expands, combines, and reduces sentences.	The writer implements most conventions. The writer: • correctly indents paragraphs most of the time. • makes occasional mechanical mistakes, but they do not hinder overall meaning.
2	The writer's ideas are somewhat organized and developed. The writer: • attempts to create an organizational structure. Ideas are difficult to follow. • attempts to group related ideas that support the opinion. • uses few words and phrases that add effect to the opinion piece. • inadequately maintains the opinion throughout the text. Text suggests the writer does not understand the stated opinion.	The writer demonstrates some understanding of the features of an opinion text. The writer: • attempts to introduce the topic. The lead is weak. • states a weak opinion about the topic. • includes one reason for the opinion. • includes some text evidence that supports the reason, but evidence is weak. • uses some linking words and phrases that connect reasons with evidence. • includes a weak concluding sentence or paragraph. • has a voice that shows some conviction about the opinion.	The writer implements some conventions. The writer: • uses parts of speech correctly some of the time. • uses grammar conventions correctly some of the time. • expands, combines, and reduces sentences some of the time. Sentence structure may confuse meaning.	The writer implements some conventions. The writer: • indents paragraphs some of the time. • makes many mechanical mistakes, and they sometimes hinder overall meaning.
1	The writer's ideas are disorganized and undeveloped. The writer: • does not attempt to create an organizational structure. • does not group related ideas. The opinion is not supported. • uses few, if any, words and phrases that add effect to the opinion piece. • does not maintain the opinion throughout the text.	The writer demonstrates little, if any, understanding of the features of an opinion text. The writer: • does not introduce the topic. There is no obvious lead. • states an unclear opinion. • includes one reason for the opinion. • includes little, if any, text evidence that supports the reason. • uses few, if any, linking words and phrases that connect reasons with evidence. • does not include a concluding sentence or paragraph. • has a voice that shows little, if any, conviction about the opinion.	The writer implements few, if any, conventions. The writer: • rarely uses parts of speech correctly. • rarely uses grammar conventions correctly. • rarely expands, combines, and reduces sentences. Sentence structure confuses meaning.	The writer implements few, if any, conventions. The writer: • does not attempt to indent paragraphs. • makes many mechanical mistakes, and they hinder overall meaning.

Opinion Checklist: Grade 5

Name _____ Date _____

Title _____

		Yes	No	Not Sure
1.	I introduce my topic with a lead that gets my readers' attention.	___	___	___
2.	I state my opinion at the beginning of my paper.	___	___	___
3.	I include reasons for my opinion based on my own thoughts about the topic.	___	___	___
4.	I group connected ideas together.	___	___	___
5.	I use evidence from the text to support my opinion.	___	___	___
6.	I use linking words and phrases to connect reasons and evidence.	___	___	___
7.	I include a concluding sentence or paragraph that makes my readers think.	___	___	___
8.	My opinion follows an organized structure.	___	___	___
9.	I choose words that make sense and make my opinion interesting.	___	___	___
10.	I do not change my opinion.	___	___	___
11.	I use my voice to show people how much I care about my opinion.	___	___	___

Quality Writing Checklist
I looked for and corrected . . .

	Yes	No	Not Sure
sentence structure (expanding, reducing, and combining).	___	___	___
parts of speech (conjunctions, prepositions, interjections).	___	___	___
grammar.	___	___	___
indented paragraphs.	___	___	___
punctuation.	___	___	___
capitalization.	___	___	___
spelling.	___	___	___

Informative/Explanatory Report Rubric: Grade 5

Score	Planning and Implementation	Evidence of Genre Characteristics	Conventions of Grammar and Usage	Conventions of Mechanics
4	The writer's ideas are well organized and well developed. The writer: • thoroughly researches the topic before writing. • includes an introduction, or lead, that grabs readers' attention. • creates a meaningful organizational structure by introducing the topic, providing general observations, and grouping related information into paragraphs or sections. • consistently varies sentence structure to facilitate clear ideas. • uses a wide variety of linking words and phrases. • uses well-chosen words and phrases and domain-specific vocabulary. • includes a strong conclusion that keeps readers thinking.	The writer demonstrates complete understanding of the features of an informational report. The writer: • thoroughly develops the topic by including accurate facts, definitions, details, and examples. • includes unique text and graphic features that support the information. • includes thoughtfully worded captions that explain each graphic feature. • includes one or more different viewpoints so readers can draw their own conclusions. • includes carefully chosen primary source documents (including quotes). • consistently maintains a formal, active voice.	The writer correctly implements all conventions. The writer: • uses parts of speech in unique ways. • uses grammar conventions in clear and concise ways. • expands, combines, and reduces sentences in unique ways that enhance meaning and style.	The writer correctly implements all conventions. The writer: • always correctly indents paragraphs. • makes no, or few, mechanical mistakes, and they do not hinder overall meaning.
3	The writer's ideas are adequately organized and developed. The writer: • researches the topic before writing. • includes an introduction, or lead. • creates an organizational structure, introduces the topic, provides general observations, and groups related information into paragraphs or sections. • varies sentence structure to facilitate clear ideas. • uses linking words and phrases to link ideas. • uses words and phrases and domain-specific vocabulary. • includes a conclusion.	The writer demonstrates an adequate understanding of the features of an informational report. The writer: • develops the topic by including accurate facts, definitions, details, and examples. • includes text and graphic features that support the information. • includes captions that explain each graphic feature. • includes one different viewpoint. • includes primary source documents. • maintains a formal, active voice.	The writer implements most conventions. The writer: • uses parts of speech correctly. • uses grammar conventions correctly. • adequately expands, combines, and reduces sentences.	The writer implements most conventions. The writer: • correctly indents paragraphs most of the time. • makes occasional mechanical mistakes, but they do not hinder overall meaning.
2	The writer's ideas are somewhat organized and developed. The writer: • does some research on the project. • includes an introduction, or lead, that is weak. • attempts to create an organizational structure. Writer attempts to group related ideas, but they are difficult to follow. • attempts to vary sentence structure. • uses some linking words and phrases. • uses some words and phrases that add effect and description. • includes a weak conclusion.	The writer demonstrates some understanding of the features of an informational report. The writer: • somewhat develops the topic by including facts, definitions, details, etc. • includes few text and graphic features to support the information. • includes some captions. Captions may not adequately address the graphic. • attempts to include one different viewpoint. The viewpoint does not necessarily connect to the topic. • includes one primary source. It may not connect to the topic and may not be a quote. • inconsistently maintains a formal, active voice.	The writer implements some conventions. The writer: • uses parts of speech correctly some of the time. • uses grammar conventions correctly some of the time. • expands, combines, and reduces sentences some of the time. Sentence structure may confuse meaning.	The writer implements some conventions. The writer: • indents paragraphs some of the time. • makes many mechanical mistakes, and they sometimes hinder overall meaning.
1	The writer's ideas are disorganized and undeveloped. The writer: • does very little research on the topic. • does not include an introduction, or lead. • does not create nor maintain an organizational structure. Ideas may be grouped, but they are difficult to follow. • does not vary sentence structure. • uses few, if any, linking words and phrases to link ideas. • uses few, if any, words and phrases that add effect and description. Writer includes few domain-specific words. • does not include a conclusion.	The writer demonstrates little, if any, understanding of the features of an informational report. The writer: • does not develop the topic. • includes few, if any, text and graphic features to support the information. • includes few, if any, captions. Captions do not necessarily explain the graphics. • does not include different viewpoints. • does not include primary source documents. • does not maintain a formal, active voice.	The writer implements few, if any, conventions. The writer: • rarely uses parts of speech correctly. • rarely uses grammar conventions correctly. • rarely expands, combines, and reduces sentences. Sentence structure confuses meaning.	The writer implements few, if any, conventions. The writer: • does not attempt to indent paragraphs. • makes many mechanical mistakes, and they hinder overall meaning.

Informative/Explanatory Report Checklist: Grade 5

Name _____ Date _____

Title _____

		Yes	No	Not Sure
1.	I researched my topic and organized my information into notes that helped me write my paper.	___	___	___
2.	I introduce my topic and use words that grab my readers' attention. I include a general observation about the topic.	___	___	___
3.	I keep my paper organized by grouping information together in a way that makes sense. I use paragraphs and sections.	___	___	___
4.	I use headings to organize my sections.	___	___	___
5.	The information in my report is accurate.	___	___	___
6.	I support my points with facts, definitions, and details.	___	___	___
7.	I include graphics to support my information.	___	___	___
8.	I include captions that explain each graphic.	___	___	___
9.	I use linking words and phrases to connect ideas.	___	___	___
10.	My report includes different viewpoints so that I do not sway my readers to think one way.	___	___	___
11.	I include a strong conclusion that keeps my readers thinking.	___	___	___
12.	I choose words that make my text interesting to read and easy to understand. I include words that connect to the topic.	___	___	___
13.	I use at least one primary source (a quote).	___	___	___
14.	I use a formal, active voice.	___	___	___

Quality Writing Checklist
I looked for and corrected . . .

	Yes	No	Not Sure
sentence structure (expanding, reducing, and combining).	___	___	___
parts of speech (conjunctions, prepositions, interjections).	___	___	___
grammar.	___	___	___
indented paragraphs.	___	___	___
punctuation.	___	___	___
capitalization.	___	___	___
spelling.	___	___	___

Narrative (Memoir) Rubric: Grade 5

Score	Planning and Implementation	Evidence of Genre Characteristics	Conventions of Grammar and Usage	Conventions of Mechanics
4	The writer's ideas are well organized and well developed. The writer: •includes events that are thoughtfully and logically sequenced. •effectively paces events to develop events and characters. •uses a variety of transition words, phrases, and clauses to manage the sequence. •uses well-chosen concrete words and phrases and sensory details to describe people, places, and events. •begins the memoir with a strong lead. •includes a strong ending that naturally makes the reader reflect on the memoir.	The writer demonstrates complete understanding of the features of a memoir. The writer: •effectively uses first person to tell the memoir. •focuses on a short period of time or several related events. •maintains a narrative form to tell the memoir (setting, plot, character development, and conflict). •effectively includes dialogue or expresses what people say in a way that brings the story to life. •uses well-chosen words to describe his/her own convictions, thoughts, and feelings as well as the actual event.	The writer correctly implements all conventions. The writer: •uses parts of speech in unique ways. •uses grammar conventions in clear and concise ways. •expands, combines, and reduces sentences in unique ways that enhance meaning and style.	The writer correctly implements all conventions. The writer: •always correctly indents paragraphs. •makes no, or few, mechanical mistakes, and they do not hinder overall meaning.
3	The writer's ideas are adequately organized and developed. The writer: •includes events that are logically sequenced. •paces events to develop events and characters. •uses transition words, phrases, and clauses to manage the sequence of events. •uses concrete words and phrases and sensory details to describe people, places, and events. •begins the memoir with a lead that grabs readers' attention. •includes an ending that makes the reader reflect on the memoir.	The writer demonstrates adequate understanding of the features of a memoir. The writer: •uses first person to tell the memoir. •focuses on a short period of time or several related events. •maintains a narrative form to tell the memoir (setting, plot, character development, and conflict). •includes dialogue or expresses what people say in a way that brings the story to life. •describes his/her own convictions, thoughts, and feelings as well as the actual event.	The writer implements most conventions. The writer: •uses parts of speech correctly. •uses grammar conventions correctly. •adequately expands, combines, and reduces sentences.	The writer implements most conventions. The writer: •correctly indents paragraphs most of the time. •makes occasional mechanical mistakes, but they do not hinder overall meaning.
2	The writer's ideas are somewhat organized and developed. The writer: •includes events that are somewhat sequenced. •attempts to pace events to develop events and characters. •uses transition words, phrases, and clauses to manage the sequence of events some of the time. •inadequately describes people, places, and events. •begins the memoir with a weak lead. •includes a weak ending.	The writer demonstrates some understanding of the features of a memoir. The writer: •uses first person to tell the memoir some of the time. •attempts to focus on a short period of time or several related events. •attempts to maintain a narrative form to tell the memoir (setting, plot, character development, and conflict). Story structure is confusing. •attempts to include dialogue or express what people say in a way that brings the story to life. •attempts to describe his/her own convictions, thoughts, and feelings as well as the actual event.	The writer implements some conventions. The writer: •uses parts of speech correctly some of the time. •uses grammar conventions correctly some of the time. •expands, combines, and reduces sentences some of the time. Sentence structure may confuse meaning.	The writer implements some conventions. The writer: •indents paragraphs some of the time. •makes many mechanical mistakes, and they sometimes hinder overall meaning.
1	The writer's ideas are disorganized and undeveloped. The writer: •includes events that are not sequenced. •does not pace events to develop the events and characters. •rarely uses transition words, phrases, and clauses to manage the sequence of events. •does not describe people, places, and events. •does not include a lead. •does not include an ending.	The writer demonstrates little, if any, understanding of the features of a memoir. The writer: •mixes first and third person. •has a focus that is unclear. •does not maintain a narrative form to tell the memoir (setting, plot, character development, and conflict). Story structure is confusing. •may attempt to include dialogue or express what people say in a way that brings the story to life. Dialogue is not used correctly or effectively. •rarely describes his/her own convictions, thoughts, and feelings as well as the actual event.	The writer implements few, if any, conventions. The writer: •rarely uses parts of speech correctly. •rarely uses grammar conventions correctly. •rarely expands, combines, and reduces sentences. Sentence structure confuses meaning.	The writer implements few, if any, conventions. The writer: •does not attempt to indent paragraphs. •makes many mechanical mistakes, and they hinder overall meaning.

Narrative (Memoir) Checklist: Grade 5

Name _____ Date _____

Title _____

		Yes	No	Not Sure
1.	My memoir has a strong lead that catches the reader's attention.	___	___	___
2.	My memoir focuses on a short period of time or several related events.	___	___	___
3.	I tell my memoir in first person.	___	___	___
4.	I tell my memoir using a narrative form. I include setting, character development, plot, and conflict.	___	___	___
5.	My memoir is logically sequenced.	___	___	___
6.	My memoir uses sequence words.	___	___	___
7.	I include specific details about the time, place, and people involved.	___	___	___
8.	I use describing words, including adjectives and adverbs, to tell my story.	___	___	___
9.	I include dialogue or express what people said.	___	___	___
10.	I pace my writing to develop characters and events.	___	___	___
11.	I include my own convictions, thoughts, and feelings.	___	___	___
12.	My memoir has a strong ending.	___	___	___

Quality Writing Checklist
I looked for and corrected . . .

	Yes	No	Not Sure
sentence structure (expanding, reducing, and combining).	___	___	___
parts of speech (conjunctions, prepositions, interjections).	___	___	___
grammar.	___	___	___
indented paragraphs.	___	___	___
punctuation.	___	___	___
capitalization.	___	___	___
spelling.	___	___	___

Argument Rubric: Grade 6

Score	Planning and Implementation	Evidence of Genre Characteristics	Conventions of Grammar and Usage	Conventions of Mechanics
4	The writer's ideas are well organized and well developed. The writer: • creates and maintains a meaningful organizational structure. • effectively groups related ideas to support the claim. • uses well-chosen words and phrases that add effect to the analytical argument. • clearly maintains a formal style and tone throughout the analytical argument.	The writer demonstrates complete understanding of the features of an analytical argument. The writer: • states a claim that shows full understanding of the topic and prompt. • clearly introduces the claim in a strong introduction. • includes multiple, logically ordered reasons for the claim based on inferences made about the topic. • includes well-chosen text evidence from credible sources that supports each reason. • uses a wide variety of transition words that connect the claim, the reasons, and the evidence. • includes an effective concluding statement that makes the reader think about the writer's ideas. • has a voice that shows strong conviction about the claim.	The writer correctly implements all conventions. The writer: • uses pronouns in unique ways that enhance the meaning and style. • uses grammar conventions in clear and concise ways. • varies sentence patterns in unique ways that enhance the meaning and style.	The writer correctly implements all conventions. The writer: • always correctly indents paragraphs. • makes no, or few, mechanical mistakes, and they do not hinder overall meaning.
3	The writer's ideas are adequately organized and developed. The writer: • creates and maintains an organizational structure. • groups related ideas to support the claim most of the time. • uses words and phrases that add effect to the analytical argument. • maintains a formal style and tone throughout most of the analytical argument.	The writer demonstrates an adequate understanding of the features of an analytical argument. The writer: • states a claim related to the topic and prompt. • introduces the claim in the first paragraph. • includes at least two multiple, logically ordered reasons for the claim. • includes text evidence from credible sources that supports each reason. • uses transition words that connect the claim, the reasons, and the evidence. • includes a concluding statement. • has a voice that shows conviction about the claim.	The writer implements most conventions. The writer: • uses pronouns correctly. • uses grammar conventions correctly. • adequately varies sentence patterns.	The writer implements most conventions. The writer: • correctly indents paragraphs most of the time. • makes occasional mechanical mistakes, but they do not hinder overall meaning.
2	The writer's ideas are somewhat organized and developed. The writer: • attempts to create an organizational structure. Ideas are difficult to follow. • attempts to group related ideas that support the claim. • uses few words and phrases that add effect to the analytical argument. • maintains a formal style and tone throughout some of the analytical argument.	The writer demonstrates understanding of the features of an analytical argument. The writer: • states a weak claim about the topic. • attempts to introduce the claim. The lead is weak. • includes one reason for the claim. • includes some text evidence that supports the reason, but evidence is weak. • uses some transition words that connect the claim, the reasons, and the evidence. • includes a weak concluding statement. • has a voice that shows some conviction about the claim.	The writer implements some conventions. The writer: • uses pronouns correctly some of the time. • uses grammar conventions correctly some of the time. • varies sentences some of the time. Sentence structure may confuse meaning.	The writer implements some conventions. The writer: • indents paragraphs some of the time. • makes many mechanical mistakes, and they sometimes hinder overall meaning.
1	The writer's ideas are disorganized and undeveloped. The writer: • does not attempt to create an organizational structure. • does not group related ideas. The claim is not supported. • uses few, if any words and phrases that add effect to the analytical argument. • does not maintain a formal style and tone in any part of the analytical argument.	The writer demonstrates little, if any, understanding of the features of an analytical argument. The writer: • states an unclear claim. • does not introduce the claim or topic. There is no obvious lead. • Includes at most one reason for the claim. • Includes little, if any, text evidence that supports the reason. • uses few, if any, transition words that connect the claim, the reasons, and the evidence. • does not include a concluding statement. • has a voice that shows little, if any, conviction about the claim.	The writer implements few, if any conventions. The writer: • rarely uses pronouns correctly. • rarely uses grammar conventions correctly. • rarely varies sentences. Sentence structure confuses meaning.	The writer implements few, if any, conventions. The writer: • does not attempt to indent paragraphs. • makes many mechanical mistakes, and they hinder overall meaning.

Argument Checklist: Grade 6

Name _____ Date _____

Title _____

		Yes	No	Not Sure
1.	I begin my argument with a strong introduction that gets my readers' attention.	___	___	___
2.	I clearly state my claim at the beginning of my paper.	___	___	___
3.	I include logical reasons to support my claim.	___	___	___
4.	I use evidence from the text to support my claim and reasons.	___	___	___
5.	I group connected ideas together.	___	___	___
6.	I use transition words and phrases to connect ideas.	___	___	___
7.	I provide a concluding statement that makes my readers think.	___	___	___
8.	My analytical argument follows an organized structure.	___	___	___
9.	I choose words to develop and support my claim and make my writing interesting.	___	___	___
10.	I maintain a consistent, formal style and tone throughout my paper.	___	___	___
11.	I use my voice to show people how much I believe my claim is correct.	___	___	___

Quality Writing Checklist
I looked for and corrected . . .

	Yes	No	Not Sure
sentence structure (varying for style and meaning).	___	___	___
improper or vague pronouns.	___	___	___
grammar.	___	___	___
indented paragraphs.	___	___	___
punctuation.	___	___	___
capitalization.	___	___	___
spelling.	___	___	___

Informative/Explanatory Report Rubric: Grade 6

Score	Planning and Implementation	Evidence of Genre Characteristics	Conventions of Grammar and Usage	Conventions of Mechanics
4	The writer's ideas are well organized and well developed. The writer: • has a strong lead that effectively introduces the topic and hooks readers. • effectively and logically sequences ideas to develop the information presented. • incorporates a variety of academic vocabulary words to make the writing more interesting. • uses well-chosen descriptive language, such as adjectives and prepositional phrases, to make writing clearer. • effectively varies sentence structure (sentence length, using similar sentence patterns for effect, combining sentences) throughout the report. • includes a strong ending that keeps readers thinking.	The writer demonstrates complete understanding of the features of a research report. The writer: • presents accurate, relevant, and compelling information. • incorporates well-chosen graphics that logically support the information. • includes well-written captions that effectively explain each graphic feature. • uses a variety of well-chosen primary sources. • incorporates at least three multiple perspectives that do not sway readers. • includes an interesting narrative story line within the informational text to effectively add voice to the report.	The writer correctly implements all conventions. The writer: • uses pronouns in unique ways that enhance the meaning and style. • uses grammar conventions in clear and concise ways. • varies sentence patterns in unique ways that enhance the meaning and style.	The writer correctly implements all conventions. The writer: • always correctly indents paragraphs. • makes no, or few, mechanical mistakes, and they do not hinder overall meaning.
3	The writer's ideas are adequately organized and developed. The writer: • has a strong lead. • logically sequences ideas to develop the information presented. • incorporates academic vocabulary words to make the writing more interesting. • uses descriptive language, such as adjectives and prepositional phrases, to make writing clearer. • varies sentence structure (sentence length, using similar sentence patterns for effect, combining sentences) throughout most of the report. • includes a strong ending.	The writer demonstrates adequate understanding of the features of a research report. The writer: • presents accurate and relevant information. • incorporates graphics that support the information. • includes captions that explain each graphic feature. • uses a variety of primary sources. • incorporates at least two multiple perspectives that do not sway readers. • includes a narrative story line within the informational text to add voice to the report.	The writer implements most conventions. The writer: • uses pronouns correctly. • uses grammar conventions correctly. • adequately varies sentence patterns.	The writer implements most conventions. The writer: • correctly indents paragraphs most of the time. • makes occasional mechanical mistakes, but they do not hinder overall meaning.
2	The writer's ideas are somewhat organized and developed. The writer: • begins with a weak lead. • attempts to logically sequence ideas to develop the information presented. • attempts to incorporate academic vocabulary words to make the writing more interesting. • attempts to use descriptive language, such as adjectives and prepositional phrases, to make writing clearer. • varies sentence structure (sentence length, using similar sentence patterns for effect, combining sentences) throughout some of the report. • includes a weak ending	The writer demonstrates some understanding of the features of a research report. The writer: • presents accurate information. • incorporates at least one graphic to support the information. • include at least one caption to explain a graphic feature. • uses primary sources. • incorporates at least two multiple perspectives. • includes a weak narrative story line within the informational text to add voice to the report.	The writer implements some conventions. The writer: • uses pronouns correctly some of the time. • uses grammar conventions correctly some of the time. • varies sentences some of the time. Sentence structure may confuse meaning.	The writer implements some conventions. The writer: • indents paragraphs some of the time. • makes many mechanical mistakes, and they sometimes hinder overall meaning.
1	The writer's ideas are disorganized and undeveloped. The writer: • does not include a lead. • does not logically sequence ideas. Organizational structure confuses meaning. • does not incorporate academic vocabulary words. • does not use descriptive language to make writing clearer. • rarely varies sentence structure (sentence length, using similar sentence patterns for effect, combining sentences). • does not include an ending.	The writer demonstrates little, if any, understanding of the features of a research report. The writer: • presents inaccurate information. • does not incorporate any graphics to support the information. • does not include any captions. • does not use primary sources. • does not incorporate multiple perspectives. • does not include a narrative story line within the informational text to add voice to the report.	The writer implements few, if any conventions. The writer: • rarely uses pronouns correctly. • rarely uses grammar conventions correctly. • rarely varies sentences. Sentence structure confuses meaning.	The writer implements few, if any, conventions. The writer: • does not attempt to indent paragraphs. • makes many mechanical mistakes, and they hinder overall meaning.

Informative/Explanatory Report Checklist: Grade 6

Name _____ Date _____

Title _____

		Yes	No	Not Sure
1.	My report has a strong lead.	___	___	___
2.	The information in my report is accurate.	___	___	___
3.	I fact-checked my information.	___	___	___
4.	I included graphics to support my information.	___	___	___
5.	I included captions that explain each graphic.	___	___	___
6.	My report includes multiple perspectives so that I do not sway my readers to think one way.	___	___	___
7.	My report is logically sequenced.	___	___	___
8.	I included academic language to make my writing more interesting.	___	___	___
9.	My report has a strong ending that keeps readers thinking.	___	___	___
10.	I included primary sources.	___	___	___
11.	I included descriptive language, such as adjectives and prepositional phrases, to make my writing clearer.	___	___	___
12.	I varied sentence structure in my research report.	___	___	___
13.	I included a narrative story line in my research report.	___	___	___

Quality Writing Checklist
I looked for and corrected . . .

	Yes	No	Not Sure
incomplete sentences.	___	___	___
subject/verb agreement.	___	___	___
correct verb tense.	___	___	___
incorrect references to money where appropriate.	___	___	___
punctuation (parentheses).	___	___	___
capitalization.	___	___	___
spelling.	___	___	___
indented paragraphs.	___	___	___

*Confer with your teacher about checklist items you are not sure you have addressed.

Narrative (Memoir) Rubric: Grade 6

Score	Planning and Implementation	Evidence of Genre Characteristics	Conventions of Grammar and Usage	Conventions of Mechanics
4	The writer's ideas are well organized and well developed. The writer: • clearly introduces a narrator and/or characters. • includes events that are thoughtfully and logically sequenced. • uses effective pacing to develop events and characters. • uses a variety of transition words, phrases, and clauses to manage the sequence. • uses precise words, descriptive details, and sensory language to describe people, places, and events. • begins with a strong lead that establishes context. • includes a strong ending that naturally makes the reader reflect on the memoir.	The writer demonstrates complete understanding of the features of a memoir. The writer: • effectively uses first person to tell the memoir. • focuses on a short period of time or several related events. • maintains a consistent narrative form to tell the memoir (setting, plot, character development, and conflict). • effectively includes dialogue or expresses what characters say in a way that brings the story to life. • uses well-chosen words to describe his/her own convictions, thoughts, and feelings as well as the actual event.	The writer correctly implements all conventions. The writer: • uses pronouns in unique ways that enhance the meaning and style. • uses grammar conventions in clear and concise ways. • varies sentence patterns in unique ways that enhance the meaning and style.	The writer correctly implements all conventions. The writer: • always correctly indents paragraphs. • makes no, or few, mechanical mistakes, and they do not hinder overall meaning.
3	The writer's ideas are adequately organized and developed. The writer: • introduces a narrator and/or characters. • includes events that are logically sequenced. • uses pacing to develop events and characters. • uses many transition words, phrases, and clauses to manage the sequence. • uses words, details, and sensory language to describe people, places, and events. • begins with a lead that establishes context. • includes an ending that makes the reader reflect on the memoir.	The writer demonstrates adequate understanding of the features of a memoir. The writer: • uses first person to tell the memoir. • focuses on a short period of time or several related events. • maintains a narrative form to tell the memoir (setting, plot, character development, and conflict). • includes dialogue or expresses what characters say in a way that brings the story to life. • describes his/her own convictions, thoughts, and feelings as well as the actual event.	The writer implements most conventions. The writer: • uses pronouns correctly. • uses grammar conventions correctly. • adequately varies sentence patterns.	The writer implements most conventions. The writer: • correctly indents paragraphs most of the time. • makes occasional mechanical mistakes, but they do not hinder overall meaning.
2	The writer's ideas are somewhat organized and developed. The writer: • somewhat introduces a narrator and/or characters. • includes events that are partially sequenced. • attempts to use pacing to develop events and characters. • uses some transition words, phrases, and clauses to manage the sequence. • inadequately describes people, places, and events. • begins with a weak lead. • includes a weak ending.	The writer demonstrates some understanding of the features of a memoir. The writer: • uses first person to tell the memoir some of the time. • attempts to focus on a short period of time or several related events. • attempts to maintain a narrative form to tell the memoir (setting, plot, character development, and conflict). • attempts to include dialogue or expresses what characters say in a way that brings the story to life. • attempts to describe his/her own convictions, thoughts, and feelings as well as the actual event.	The writer implements some conventions. The writer: • uses pronouns correctly some of the time. • uses grammar conventions correctly some of the time. • varies sentences some of the time. Sentence structure may confuse meaning.	The writer implements some conventions. The writer: • indents paragraphs some of the time. • makes many mechanical mistakes, and they sometimes hinder overall meaning.
1	The writer's ideas are disorganized and undeveloped. The writer: • does not introduce a narrator and/or characters. • includes events that are not sequenced. • does not use pacing to develop events and characters. • uses few, if any, transition words, phrases, and clauses to manage the sequence. • does not describe people, places, and events. • does not include a lead. • does not include an ending.	The writer demonstrates little, if any, understanding of the features of a memoir. The writer: • mixes first and third person. • has a focus that is unclear. • does not maintain a narrative form to tell the memoir (setting, plot, character development, and conflict). Story structure is confusing. • may attempt to include dialogue or express what characters say. Dialogue is not used correctly or effectively. • rarely describes his/her own convictions, thoughts, and feelings as well as the actual event.	The writer implements few, if any conventions. The writer: • rarely uses pronouns correctly. • rarely uses grammar conventions correctly. • rarely varies sentences. Sentence structure confuses meaning.	The writer implements few, if any, conventions. The writer: • does not attempt to indent paragraphs. • makes many mechanical mistakes, and they hinder overall meaning.

Narrative (Memoir) Checklist: Grade 6

Name _____ Date _____

Title _____

		Yes	No	Not Sure
1.	My memoir has a strong lead.	——	——	——
2.	My memoir focuses on one part of my life.	——	——	——
3.	My memoir focuses on events the way I remember them.	——	——	——
4.	I included thoughts and feelings about the events that explain why they are important to me.	——	——	——
5.	I included specific details about the time, place, and people involved.	——	——	——
6.	My memoir is logically sequenced.	——	——	——
7.	I included my current views about these events.	——	——	——
8.	I included dialogue.	——	——	——
9.	My memoir has a strong ending that makes readers think.	——	——	——
10.	My memoir is written using first person narrative.	——	——	——
11.	I included dependent clauses and demonstrative pronouns to make my writing clearer.	——	——	——
12.	I included descriptive words to tell about people, places, events, and ideas.	——	——	——
13.	I included compound, complex, and simple sentences to make my writing more interesting.	——	——	——

Quality Writing Checklist
I looked for and corrected . . .

	Yes	No	Not Sure
incomplete sentences.	——	——	——
subject/verb agreement.	——	——	——
correct verb tense.	——	——	——
correct abbreviations where applicable.	——	——	——
correct punctuation.	——	——	——
capitalization (song titles).	——	——	——
spelling.	——	——	——
indented paragraphs.	——	——	——

*Confer with your teacher about checklist items you are not sure you have addressed.

Using Informal Assessments for Parent/Teacher Communication

Parent-teacher conferences are a dynamic way for teachers and parents to discuss the academic, behavioral, and social well-being of students. Conferences have many purposes such as, setting goals together, recognizing strengths and needs, and determining ways to measure progress for the school year. Including students in the conferencing process encourages both the student and teacher to share with parents the targeted goals of reading, writing, speaking, and listening.

1. Develop a strategic plan with each student for reading, writing, speaking, and listening.

2. The focus of each conference should be on the individual student and his/her own progress and behaviors.

3. Gather all data from multiple sources, including informal assessment materials, such as:

   • Anecdotal records
   • Results from the level screeners
   • Results from running records
   • Small-group observation checklists and records
   • Retelling assessments
   • Writing assessment frames

4. Include the student in the conference.

5. Be positive and focused on plans to correct any problems you and the parents and/or the student agree upon.

Year-at-a-Glance Planning Calendar

Teacher Name _____ Grade _____ Level _____

Notes:	August	September	October
November	**December**	**January**	**February**
March	**April**	**May**	**June**

Month-at-a-Glance Planning Calendar

Teacher Name _____ Grade _____ Level _____

	Monday	Tuesday	Wednesday	Thursday	Friday
Week of:					
Week of:					
Week of:					
Week of:					

Week-at-a-Glance Planning Calendar

Teacher Name _____   Grade _____   Level _____

	Monday	Tuesday	Wednesday	Thursday	Friday
Progress-Monitoring Assessments					
Individual Reading Conferences					

Anecdotal Notes

Teacher Name _____

Grade _____

Level _____
